When Gao Xingjian was crowned Nobel Laureate in 2000, it was the first time in the hundred-year history of the Nobel Prize that this honor had been awarded to an author for a body of work written in Chinese. The same year, American readers embraced Mabel Lee's translation of Gao's lyrical and autobiographical novel *Soul Mountain,* making it a national best seller. Gao's plays, novels, and short fiction have won the Chinese expatriate an international following and a place among the world's greatest living writers.

The bold and extraordinary essays in this volume—all beautifully translated by sinologist Mabel Lee—include Gao's Nobel Lecture ("The Case for Literature"), "Literature as Testimony: The Search for Truth," "Cold Literature," "Literature and Metaphysics: About *Soul Mountain,*" and "The Necessity of Loneliness," as well as other essays. These essays embody an argument for literature as a universal human

the case for literature

GAO XINGJIAN, *Early Winter*, 1991
Ink on paper
50 x 56.5 cm

the case for literature

GAO XINGJIAN

TRANSLATED FROM THE CHINESE BY MABEL LEE

YALE UNIVERSITY PRESS • *New Haven* and *London*

This collection first published in the United States in 2007
by Yale University Press.
This collection first published in Australia in 2006
by HarperCollins*Publishers* Australia Pty Limited.

Designed by Katy Wright, HarperCollins Design Studio

Set in 10.5/15 Galliard by Kirby Jones

Printed in the United States of America.

Library of Congress Control Number: 2006933452

ISBN 978-0-300-12421-7 (cloth : alk. paper)

A catalogue record for this book is available from the British Library.

The paper in this book meets the guidelines for permanence and durability
of the Committee on Production Guidelines for Book Longevity of the
Council on Library Resources.

10 9 8 7 6 5 4 3 2 1

Contents

Introduction

Contextualising 2000 Nobel Laureate Gao Xingjian

GAO XINGJIAN (born 4 January 1940, Ganzhou, Jiangxi province, China) achieved celebrity status at home and abroad when his first two plays, *Alarm Signal* (1982) and *Bus Stop* (1983), were staged at the People's Art Theatre in Beijing to wildly ecstatic audiences.

It was just a few years earlier, in 1976, that the death of Mao Zedong had ended the Cultural Revolution (1966–1976), a decade during which writers were singled out for persecution. While older, published writers were still traumatised by their experiences, Gao was among a cohort of younger, unpublished writers who audaciously tested the still-volatile political climate by publishing works that contravened Mao's literary guidelines, established in Yan'an in 1942 and rigorously policed throughout the Cultural Revolution.

Yet in order to understand the context of Gao Xingjian's work fully, it is necessary to go back even further in China's history, to the intellectual revolution known as the May Fourth Movement (1915–1919) — named after the student protest march in Beijing in 1919 — that led to the emergence of modern Chinese literature.

During this period young Chinese intellectuals seized the mantle of moral authority from their elders, judging them to have failed the nation. They blamed China's past literature for perpetuating moribund cultural traditions that hindered modernisation, and demanded a new culture based on science and democracy that would help bring the nation into the modern world.

The most eloquent spokespeople for this movement were writers who, while having a solid grounding in classical Chinese literature, were also widely read in European literature. The literature they developed was substantially different from established traditions: it was heavily influenced by European literature, it was written in the spoken language instead of the classical language, and it dealt with contemporary issues.

This new writing was published in the numerous avant-garde magazines of the period alongside translations from Nietzsche's *Thus Spake Zarathustra* and introductory essays on Nietzsche. Intoxicated by Nietzsche's "Superman" and his pronouncement "God is dead!", May Fourth writers became the heroes of Chinese youth, and many of them also came to see themselves as heroes whose writings could help save the nation.

However, the romantic idealism of May Fourth ended with the Paris Peace Conference of 1919, when it was revealed that secret treaties amongst the Allies had already ceded German-held territories in China to Japan. Many Chinese intellectuals had worshipped Western democracies for decades, and the sense of betrayal they experienced was profound.

On 4 May 1919, high school and university students in Beijing staged a march to call upon the authorities not to sign the Paris Peace Treaty. They were met by mounted police wielding bayoneted rifles. The beatings and arrests that followed led to mass protests all over the country. However, after a few months of continued beatings, arrests and even executions, protester numbers dwindled to mainly hard-core activists, amongst whom many were communists. In 1921 the Chinese Communist Party was founded.

To Chinese intellectuals faced with the realities of those times, it seemed that individual protest was futile and that unified political action was the only way to save the nation. During the 1920s and 1930s large numbers of patriotic intellectuals were drawn into abrogating their rights as individuals and becoming involved in politics. Meanwhile, Japan escalated its territorial thrust into China, culminating in full-scale invasion in 1937. China's War of Resistance against Japan ended in 1945, but was followed by civil war. The victory of the Communists, and the retreat of the Nationalists to Taiwan, made way for the founding of the People's Republic of China by Mao Zedong in 1949.

Under Mao, political control extended to all aspects of Chinese life, including literature and the arts: literary production, like all other modes of production, should serve the masses. The designated role of literature was to educate the people, and in all literary representations characters had to be portrayed as unambiguously good or bad. The "good" characters were to serve as role models for the masses, while anyone seen to be behaving like the "bad" characters was to be reported immediately to the authorities, who were the arbiters of what was "good" and "bad". These guidelines were institutionalised with the founding of the People's Republic of China.

Refusing to conform to Mao's guidelines for literature, Gao had no alternative but to write in secret. His voracious reading habit and his studies at the Beijing Foreign Languages Institute (from which he graduated with a major in French literature in 1962) allowed him to develop as a writer. He was subsequently assigned work as an editor and translator at the Foreign Languages Press, and at the outbreak of the Cultural Revolution he burned a suitcase full of manuscripts — ten plays and a large number of short stories, poems and essays — rather than risk having them found by rampaging Red Guards and used as evidence against him.

Gao came under investigation for his activities as the leader of a Red Guard group, but before a campaign was properly launched against him he fled to a remote mountain village, and resigned himself to spending the rest of his life working as a peasant in the fields rather than risk arrest and imprisonment.

In that period (1970–1975), he again began to write in secret, but not before he had made elaborate preparations that would allow him to quickly hide what he was writing if necessary. During this bleak era, when people in China could not articulate their thoughts without endangering their own lives, Gao found that writing was his only salvation. It was only through writing down his thoughts and feelings that he could affirm the existence of his private self.

He was able to return to Beijing in 1975, and resumed his position at the Foreign Languages Press. The following year, the Cultural Revolution came to an end and there was cautious optimism in the literary world as China, after decades of isolation, gradually opened itself up to outside influences. The publishing world was quick to respond to the less repressive political climate, and new literary magazines proliferated. In 1979 Gao travelled to France as the official interpreter for a delegation of Chinese writers headed by the veteran writer Ba Jin, and in 1980 he went to Italy as a member of a delegation of Chinese writers.

From 1980, at the age of forty, he began to see his writings published. During 1980 and 1981 his publications included two novellas, *Stars on a Cold Night* (1980) and *A Pigeon Called Red Beak* (1981); two scholarly critiques of modern French literature, "The French Modernist People's Poet Prévert and his *Words*" (1980) and "Modern French Literature's Agony" (1980); two prose essays, "Ba Jin in Paris" (1980) and "Italian Caprice" (1981); and two short stories, "Friends" (1981) and "Rain, Snow and Other" (1981). Most significantly, his scholarly work *Preliminary Explorations Into the Art of Modern Fiction*, which had been serialised in the Guangzhou-based monthly *Jottings* in 1980, was published as a book in 1981.

In this treatise, Gao discusses how the advent of cinema and other technological changes have influenced the way people appreciate fiction, and claims that this has made it necessary for writers to pay greater attention to literary techniques and language use. Gao notes that new life had been breathed into the genre through the use of flashbacks and stream of consciousness in writings in the West, but that these techniques were virtually unknown in China in the early 1980s. He systematically introduces each of them, giving examples and demonstrating how and why they are effective. The techniques used by the great novelists of China and Russia are also compared and discussed. But the authorities would not have missed his patently subversive proposal that fiction is ineffectual if it preaches, and that a successful work of fiction is premised on freedom — for the author, the characters and the reader.

In 1981 Gao was reassigned to work as a writer at the People's Art Theatre. (He deals with this period of his life in "Wilted Chrysanthemums", one of the essays in the current collection. This essay is an important archival document on the complexities of China's literary world at that time, and provides a contextual basis for understanding his intensely serious commitment to literature.) In 1982 his play *Alarm Signal* was staged ten times at the People's Art Theatre as "experimental theatre". This meant that audiences were restricted to literary and art circles. In the early 1980s, although the Cultural Revolution had ended, politics continued to exert an invasive influence on the creative arts. The classification "experimental theatre" was created as an attempt to get around this difficulty.

The narrative of *Alarm Signal* is simple: it tells of how a train robbery is thwarted because one of the villains has a change of heart. Gao used techniques that deviated from established theatre practice in China, such as flashbacks, and changes in perspective; the emphasis was on the psychology of the characters. Members of the audience were agog with

5

excitement because of the ambiguity of "good" and "bad" in the characters of the play, and because they themselves had to make up their own minds about the morality of the characters. For the custodians of Mao's guidelines in the Chinese Writers' Association, however, the play was problematic, although at the time no action was taken. Public performances followed, and the French newspaper *Le Monde* declared to the world that avant-garde theatre had arrived in Beijing.

During that year three of Gao's short stories, "On the Road", "On the Sea" and "Twenty-five Years Later", were also published, adding to his credentials as an innovative writer of fiction. In addition, *Preliminary Explorations Into the Art of Modern Fiction* was reprinted, and the fact that several established writers had applauded the work in literary publications brought it to the attention of the authorities.

A shift in power in the upper echelons of government meant that by early 1983 the Chinese Writers' Association was able to launch two mass meetings to attack a book by a "minor writer" that was challenging the nation's socialist–realist literary traditions and having a detrimental effect on young writers. Being that "minor writer", Gao was ordered to attend. What the organisers had not anticipated was that well-known writers would come forward on both occasions to speak in defence of the book.

Gao was emboldened by this to proceed with the staging of his next play, *Bus Stop*. The play is about a motley group of people at a bus stop waiting for a bus. Buses go past but none of them stop; years go by but they continue to wait. While they wait, what passes through their minds and what they say and do are under scrutiny. The only character to take decisive action is a latecomer on the scene, Silent Man, who walks off after a short wait. Like *Alarm Signal*, *Bus Stop* was staged as experimental theatre, but was banned after its tenth performance — although two special performances were subsequently ordered to enable people to write criticisms of the play for the major literary publications.

The Oppose Spiritual Pollution campaign had been launched, and Gao was one of its first casualties. His *Preliminary Explorations Into the Art of Modern Fiction* was now banned, along with *Bus Stop*, and he was duly entered on a blacklist of names that was circulated to publishers. Nonetheless, before the ban on his publications became effective that year, a large number of writings went into print. These included five short stories, "Garland of Flowers", "The Temple", "Mother", "On the Other Side of the River" and "The Shoemaker and His Daughter"; and eleven essays discussing Gao's ideas on the writing of fiction and drama, "On the Relationship Between Modern Fiction and the Reader", "Cold Sentiment and Anti-sentiment", "Simplicity and Purity", "About Perspective in Theatre", "Theatrical Experimentation with Polyphony", "Devices in Modern Theatre", "On the Nature of the Stage", "On Theatricality", "Action and Process", "Time and Space" and "Suppositionality".

In the course of the events surrounding *Bus Stop*, Gao was diagnosed with lung cancer, so he took sick leave and travelled south to stay with his brother. There, a second examination confirmed that diagnosis, but a visit to a specialist two weeks later made it clear beyond doubt that a wrong diagnosis had been given. That being the case, he was required to return at once to Beijing.

There was talk in the upper echelons of sending him to a prison farm in Qinghai province for "retraining", but he did not to wait to be sent. Instead, he immediately fled Beijing, leaving a note at his workplace that he was off to the forest highlands in the far southwest of the country to carry out research into the lives of the woodcutters. He spent the next five months travelling to the source of the Yangtze River then leisurely following it down to the sea. As a fugitive from the authorities, he kept to the margins of Han Chinese society, living much of the time on nature reserves and amongst minority nationalities.

These months of solitude allowed him to reflect on human existence, society and history, as well as on his own life. They also gave him the time and the freedom to think about the long novel that he had begun to plan the previous year. It would be a "modern" Chinese novel, and he would write it purely for his own enjoyment, because it would have no prospect of publication in China. He would take the manuscript of this novel with him to France at the end of 1987, and it would subsequently be published in Taiwan as *Soul Mountain* (1990).

Soul Mountain was an experiment on a grand scale. To write it meant first finding an appropriate form of language. Gao felt that the written Chinese language currently in use had become corrupted by the grammar of Western languages. This was the result of the enormous number of "hard" (that is, literal) translations of Western writings that had been published since the early years of the twentieth century as part of China's desperate bid to modernise. In his opinion, Westernised Chinese grammar had divested the written language of its auditory appeal, its inherent musicality. By rigorously examining the language, he worked out strategies for purging his writing of corrupting elements that had crept into the written language, and to ensure that he invested auditory appeal in what he wrote, he systematically tape-recorded what he wanted to say before writing it down.

In *Soul Mountain*, Gao drew on his extensive understanding of narrative techniques employed in the fiction of both the East and the West. As in all of his writing, it was the psychological dimension of human behaviour that he sought to explore, but in the case of *Soul Mountain*, it was his own psychology that he held up for scrutiny.

The main subject of the novel is Gao's five-month journey in the Chinese hinterland, after fleeing Beijing and the political campaign that had been launched against him. To relieve his loneliness on this solitary journey, the fictional narrator "I" creates the character "You" so that he will have someone to talk to. Since "You" is a reflection of "I", "You" is also assailed by loneliness, so he creates "She" as a companion. While "I" narrates what he observes in the many places he visits, "You" and "She" travel together on a spiritual journey. "She" reawakens the lust for sex in "You", and they tell one another stories as they journey together to Soul Mountain. Through the characters "You" and "She", Gao explores male–female relationships, and he articulates the view that whereas women love their partners in sex, men have more of a propensity for lust than love.

Gao had experimented with using pronouns to provide different perspectives on the psychology of a single character in his short stories, and he found he was able to sustain this in *Soul Mountain*. His use of pronouns would become a defining feature of his later plays, and in his second autobiographical novel, *One Man's Bible* (1999), it allowed him the psychological space to scrutinise his own thinking and behaviour throughout the Cultural Revolution.

During his absence from Beijing, Gao was denounced for promoting the modernist literature of the decadent capitalist West. There was a nervous anxiety in the literary world that the Oppose Spiritual Pollution campaign would lead back to the repressive times of the Cultural Revolution. However, the campaign petered out towards the end of 1983 and friends advised Gao that it was safe to return.

In 1984, Gao's manuscripts that had been shelved during the previous year were released. His publications that year included *Highlights of Modern Opera*, in four parts ("The Imitator", "Getting Out of the Rain", "A Tough Journey by

Foot" and "Habala Pass"); a short story, "Flower Bud"; and an essay, "My Views on Drama". His novella *A Pigeon Called Red Beak* was also published as a book. Meanwhile, *Bus Stop* was staged in Yugoslavia and broadcast on radio in Hungary.

Gao's 1985 publications include *Collected Plays by Gao Xingjian*; two new plays, *Soliloquy* and *Wild Man*; four short stories, "Disgrace", "In the Park", "The Accident" and "Untitled"; and two essays, "*Wild Man* and Me" and "Brecht and Me". For the first time he held an exhibition of his Chinese ink paintings in Beijing. He also travelled by invitation to Germany and France, to give lectures and readings and to exhibit his paintings. While in Europe, he went on to give readings in the United Kingdom, Denmark and Austria.

However, on returning to Beijing for the staging of *Wild Man*, he found that the actors were being cautioned against performing in any more of his plays. *Wild Man* would be the last of his plays to be staged in China; in 1986 his play *The Other Shore* was banned at rehearsal. It became apparent that the Chinese Writers' Association was waging a vendetta against him.

At the end of 1987 he succeeded in relocating to Paris, where, by selling his Chinese ink paintings for a living, he was able to devote himself to writing without harassment and without having to exercise self-censorship.

After settling in Paris, Gao Xingjian published *Soul Mountain* and *One Man's Bible*, and a collection of seventeen short stories, *Buying a Fishing Rod for My Grandfather* (1988). He also wrote or revised the plays contained in his collection *Six Volumes of Plays by Gao Xingjian* (1995): *The Other Shore* (1986), *Fleeing* (1990), *Between Life and Death* (1991), *Romance of "The Classic of Mountains and Seas"* (1993), *Dialogue and Rebuttal* (1993), *Netherworld* (1995) and *Nocturnal Wanderer* (1995). His publication *Weekend Quartet* (1996) contained the play *Weekend Quartet* as well as a piece for dance and two poems. He also wrote French versions of three of his plays, *Between Life and Death* (1993), *Nocturnal Wanderer* (1995) and *Weekend Quartet* (1998). In the same period, through solo exhibitions, and the publication of books of his paintings and essays on his aesthetics and painting, Gao established his credentials as an artist.

In 1989, a little over a year after Gao had settled in Paris, Beijing students began to gather in Tiananmen Square to petition the Chinese authorities to put an end to bureaucratic profiteering and to bring about democratic changes. Significantly, it was the tenth anniversary of the Democracy Wall Movement of 1979, and the seventieth anniversary of the May Fourth Movement of 1919. Emotions were running high amongst the protesters. Protracted internal struggles at the highest levels of the Communist Party led to an indecisive response from the authorities, and as students from all parts of the country flocked to Tiananmen Square, an atmosphere of optimistic festivity developed.

The military crackdown in the early hours of 4 June evacuated the students from the Square. A massacre of hundreds of protesters was followed by arrests, executions, beatings and imprisonments.

Like the rest of the world, Gao watched these events with horror on televised news broadcasts. He tore up his Chinese passport and applied for political asylum in France. In interviews for French television, the magazine *Le Sud* and the Italian daily *La Stampa*, he angrily denounced the actions of the Chinese authorities. In September he finally completed his novel *Soul Mountain*, which he had worked on for seven years, and sent it off for publication. This for him was a symbol of his break with the country where he had spent the first forty-seven years of his life.

Gao had agreed to write a play about the events in China for an American theatre company, and in October he wrote

Fleeing. (He discusses this in his essay "About *Fleeing*".) The company arranged for a translation, but subsequently asked for changes because there were no student heroes. Gao declined to make any changes, paid the translator and withdrew his manuscript, stating that while he was in China the Communist Party could not persuade him to alter his manuscripts, so an American theatre company certainly would not.

When *Fleeing* was published at the beginning of 1990, it upset members of the Chinese Democracy Movement because it accused the student leaders of infantile behaviour: in failing to assess their opponents and work out an exit plan, they had caused countless unnecessary deaths. The play also incensed the Chinese authorities because of its claim that a massacre had taken place in the Square. But the authorities were even more critical of the carnal lust of the play's three characters, Young Man (a student), Woman (a broadcaster) and Middle-aged Man (the persona of the author) — especially the promiscuity of the woman. Yet Gao had no intention of writing a play for a particular political group; as always, his primary concern was the portrayal of human psychology and behaviour.

The play is without doubt an indictment of the brutal massacre of unarmed protesters in Tiananmen Square. It opens with the student and the woman fleeing from the Square into a disused warehouse to hide as the strafing of machine guns and assault rifles is heard nearby. The woman discovers that her skirt is covered in blood: the woman who had been running alongside her was shot in the stomach. Then she sees something on the student's head and asks if he has been wounded. When he tells her that it is the brain matter of someone who was shot in the head right in front of him, she is on the verge of hysteria. She cannot stand the smell of the blood on her and wants to scream. The student tells her to take off her skirt and calm down. She does so, but clings to the student, and before long feelings of sexual lust emerge. They are interrupted by the arrival of the middle-aged man.

The three of them assess their situation. It is a little more than an hour before daybreak, when they know raids will begin and they will be flushed out of hiding and arrested, imprisoned or maybe even executed. The student adopts a heroic stance and proclaims that despite this setback the people's struggle for democracy will go on. The final victory will be theirs, even if blood has to be spilled. Although the middle-aged man was also in the Square with the students, he argues that it was folly to mobilise a mass movement that pitched soft-drink bottles and bricks against machine guns and tanks. It was suicidal.

The student becomes impatient with the middle-aged man's talk; he decides to make a run for it and urges the other two to follow. However, as soon as he is out the door there is rifle fire, and it is assumed that the student has been killed. The middle-aged man and the woman talk erratically, sometimes recalling fragments of childhood memories. In the eerie loneliness of imminent death they sublimate their terror through the comfort of one another's bodies.

Gao's criticism of the student through the middle-aged man is a repudiation of Nietzsche. One's perception of oneself as a hero — a Superman — inflates the ego to such an extent that rational thinking becomes impossible. With crowds of such heroes fired by righteous indignation, a form of mass hysteria can be induced through totems, even those as noble as nationalism or democracy.

Gao later found confirmation of his analysis of crowd behaviour in an observation made by French philosopher Henri Laborit in his book *Ode to Fleeing* (1976): once protest becomes organised, the protester is reduced to being a follower of the organiser, and the only escape is to flee. In "About *Fleeing*" Gao broadens Laborit's thesis, positing that life is continual fleeing — from political oppression, from others, and even from the self. There are external pressures exerted by politics, social customs, fashions and the will of others, but mankind's misfortunes also derive from the self. The self is not God; it cannot be suppressed, but there is no need to worship it. He writes: "Once the self has been awakened, it is this that one cannot flee; this is the tragedy of modern man." Gao sees this truth as being central to classical Greek tragedy, and it was for this reason that he wrote *Fleeing* as "pure tragedy".

Gao has no objection to the individual who makes political statements and even participates in politics, but he is strongly opposed to literature that distorts truth for some cause or end, and he argues consistently for literature that is "the voice of the individual", that is "without isms", and that is "cold literature". His essays on these topics were published as a collection in *Without Isms* (1996) and brought to a conclusion his reflections on the student protests in Tiananmen, the writing of *Fleeing* and the reactions to the play.

In the same year Gao started the painful journey of revisiting the Cultural Revolution through the writing of his novel *One Man's Bible*, which he would complete in 1999. Like his first novel *Soul Mountain*, it is autobiographical fiction, and it represents his clean break with China: in 1997, in the course of writing the novel, he became a French citizen.

In *One Man's Bible*, Gao's repudiation of Nietzsche is again central: it allows him to understand his own behaviour, as well as the strategy Mao Zedong used to coerce an entire population into submission. Gao had unwittingly allowed himself to be drawn into politics at the beginning of the Cultural Revolution when he produced posters to protest against the brutal beating of senior colleagues at his workplace by Red Guards. As a result he had been treated as a hero. Believing he was carrying out a sacred mission, he had joined a rival Red Guard group, which he had immediately been pushed into leading. After that, there had been no way of retreat apart from fleeing.

In the novel Mao is portrayed as a megalomaniacal dictator who believes that he is a Superman, and his tyrannical grip on power is ensured by his deployment of lesser Supermen entrusted with the heroic mission of carrying out his will. In writing his two autobiographical novels *Soul Mountain* and *One Man's Bible*, Gao may be said to have expunged the grief that he had experienced on a number of levels during the Cultural Revolution, particularly his grief at perceiving his own self being progressively snuffed out.

Gao's profound loathing of Nietzsche, evident in both *Fleeing* and *One Man's Bible*, is based on an understanding of the man and his works that is far from superficial. When the Cultural Revolution ended, a Nietzsche craze, mirroring the earlier craze of the May Fourth era, had broken out in the Chinese intellectual world. Peaking during the mid–1980s, it had resulted in the publication of hundreds of articles on the philosopher, as well as new translations of his writings. In the year or so before he left China, Gao had read Hong Kong editions of all of Nietzsche's major works. From the 1990s Nietzsche is mentioned unfavourably in several of Gao's essays: "Parisian Notes" (1991), and five of the essays included in this present volume: "The Voice of the Individual" (1993), "Without Isms" (1993), "Author's Preface to *Without Isms*" (1995), "The Case for Literature" (2000) and "Literature as Testimony: The Search for Truth" (2001).

In 2000, Gao was awarded the Nobel Prize for Literature, "for an oeuvre of universal validity, bitter insights and linguistic ingenuity, which has opened new paths for the Chinese novel and drama". By then his major works had been published in Chinese, French, Swedish and English, and a number of his plays had been staged in China, Yugoslavia, France, Sweden,

Austria, Poland, Germany, Japan, Australia, the United States, Italy, Romania, Hong Kong, Taiwan and the Ivory Coast.

The City of Marseilles designated 2003 as Gao Xingjian Year, and Gao's French play *The Interrogator of Death* (2003) was staged as one of the events at Marseilles' Gymnasium Theatre. (Gao rewrote it in Chinese the following year.) Set in a museum of contemporary art, the play is a powerful attack on Nietzsche and modernity, particularly contemporary art, as well as a summary of Gao's views on life and death. Two actors dressed in black, Actor A (a neurotic old man) and Actor B (a sombre, older man), present a soliloquy from two perspectives, which doubles its impact. Actor B is Actor A's inner voice. Both comment on each other's actions; they observe one another but their eyes do not meet.

Actor A enters the museum and later finds that he has been locked inside. He looks at the installations of cigarette butts, urinals, used toilet paper and the like, and thinks that if all this rubbish can be exhibited, and critiques using the latest jargon be written up in catalogues, then he too deserves to be one of the exhibits. He is amazed by his own genius in thinking of displaying himself as a live person. He will become a world celebrity; he will be just like a soccer star, without having to undergo all those years of rigorous training. Admitting to being narcissistic — no different from everyone else — he is excited by the prospect of being listed in art history books, of becoming the subject of critical analysis, of being repeatedly deconstructed. He will win more acclaim than any of the other artworks on display, and will become the topic of endless discussion among art critics.

Through the lips of this neurotic old man, Gao charges the modernity spawned by Nietzsche with having created a continuing drive for people to be trendsetters solely in order to be sensational, even if it is through doing something futile like masturbating in front of a camera. The trend of subverting

one's predecessors and debunking all that is old is the same as a
father who teaches his son to shoot, then is shot by the son so
that the son will become head of the family. Having announced
the death of God, people charge forward wanting to be God
themselves. Actor A reflects on life and on his abhorrence of
being controlled, even by old age or death. This leads him to
think up an even more brilliant way to be displayed in the art
museum: he commits suicide right there and then.

Throughout the play Actor B comments on Actor A's
soliloquy, sympathising with him, praising him, ridiculing him,
but finally guiding him to take that final step. His words
heighten the absurdity of Actor A's actions and provide much
wry humour. (Humour is in fact an element present in most of
Gao's plays, introduced with great deftness to significantly
increase the very gravity of the issues being addressed. In
Fleeing, for example, there are touches of humour that are
memorable for this reason.)

In the previous year, while directing rehearsals in Taipei for
his "modern" Peking Opera *Snow in August* (2002), Gao had
collapsed and been hospitalised. He had recovered sufficiently
to direct the premiere performance in December, before
returning to Paris where he directed performances of his play
Weekend Quartet at Comédie Française. In February and March
of 2003 he had two bypass operations. In June, while directing
rehearsals for *The Interrogator of Death*, he collapsed again, but
went on to direct the premiere of the play in September 2003.

However, his failing health and stern warnings from his
doctor now forced him to take stock of his health. He found
that reading anything serious instantly raised his blood
pressure; it was only possible for him to write poetry or paint,
and for little more than a few hours each day. Despite these
limitations, several of his paintings were hung at the
International Fair for Contemporary Art (FIAC) in Paris in

2003 and 2004. Gao also had a number of solo exhibitions, notably those at Claude Bernard Gallery in Paris and the Centre for Contemporary Culture in Barcelona, both in 2004; and at Frank Pages Art Gallery in Baden and Singapore Art Museum in 2005.

By February 2005 Gao was strong enough to direct the staging of *Snow in August* at the Marseilles Opera House. At the International Gao Xingjian Symposium at the University of Provence that had been organised to coincide with the stage production, he received his Honorary Doctorate from Taiwan National University.

By the start of 2006 his health had significantly improved. In February he produced a "cinematic poem" in French, *Silhouette if not Shadow*; in March he travelled to the Venice Biennale to attend two performances of his play *Dialogue and Rebuttal*, with the actors from the original French production; and in April he attended the Twenty-fourth International Fair for Contemporary Art in Brussels, where Claude Bernard Gallery exhibited a significant number of his recent paintings. He has just completed four video lectures for the Faculty of Humanities of National Taiwan University: "The Place of the Writer", "Art in Fiction", "Possibilities in Theatre" and "The Aesthetics of the Artist".

Further mention must be made of Gao's painting, because it is this that now dominates his creative life. He had originally intended to study art at university, but the prospect of painting only works of propaganda led him to study French literature instead. However, his love of painting did not diminish. He initially wanted to create works like the European masters, but after visiting the galleries and museums of France and Italy in 1979 and 1980, he could see that it would take more than a lifetime to realise this ambition. It was at this point that he turned from oils, which he had used from childhood, to Chinese ink painting. Like his writings, his ink painting is not bound by traditional practice. Instead, he has introduced the light and perspective of European art into his work, and has successfully expanded the aesthetic potential of Chinese ink painting. His works are invariably depictions of the inner mind, and convey an acute sense of loneliness and distance.

Gao's first solo exhibition at the People's Art Theatre in Beijing in 1985 was followed by exhibitions in towns and cities throughout France (Paris, Marseilles, Metz, L'Isle-sur-la Sorgue, Bayonne, Aix-en-Provence, Caen, Bourges, Rambouillet, Wattrelos, Avignon, Lille, Cassis and Bordeaux) as well as cities in various parts of the world, including Vienna, New York, London, Stockholm, Malmö, Pozna´n, Luxembourg, Hong Kong, Madrid, Barcelona, Mons, Brussels, Berlin, Aachen, Baden-Baden, Taipei and Singapore. His paintings have been collected by public institutions such as the Morat Institute for Art and Art History (Freiberg), the Leibniz Society for Cultural Exchange (Berlin), the East Asian Museum (Stockholm), the Krapperup Art Museum (Malmö), the Bourges House of Culture (Bourges), the Nantes Artothèque (Nantes), the Taipei Fine Art Museum (Taipei), the National History Museum (Taipei), the Théâtre Molière (Paris), The Nobel Foundation (Stockholm), the City of Marseilles and the Chinese University of Hong Kong.

Gao has now made his mark as an artist, playwright, choreographer, director, novelist and filmmaker. His work has brought him many honours in addition to the Nobel Prize. He was awarded the title Chevalier for Art and Literature in France in 1992, and in 2000 that of Chevalier in the Legion of Honour. In 2000 he also won the Italian Feronia Literary Prize. He received three Honorary Doctorates in 2001, from Sun Yat-sen University in Taiwan, the Chinese University of Hong Kong and the University of Provence. In France, he was invited to serve as a Member of the Committee for Lectures of the

Comédie Française in 2002, and was elected a member of the Universal Academy of Cultures in 2003.

*   *   *

Gao's 2000 Nobel Lecture was called "The Case for Literature", and this is the title of the present book of essays chosen by him for publication in English. "Literature as Testimony: The Search for Truth" was presented at the Nobel Centennial Symposium in 2001. Both of these lectures were first published in Chinese, Swedish, French and English on the Swedish Academy website. "The Case for Literature" was subsequently published in *Dictionary of Literary Biography: Yearbook 2000*, edited by Matthew J. Bruccoli (Bruccoli Clark Layman, Detroit, San Francisco, London, Boston and Woodbridge, Connecticut, 2001), *World Literature Today* 75.1 (2001) and *Publications of the Modern Language Association of America (PMLA)*, 116.3 (2001). "Literature as Testimony: The Search for Truth" was subsequently published in *Witness Literature: Proceedings of the Nobel Centennial Symposium*, edited by Horace Engdahl (New Scientific, New Jersey, London, Singapore and Hong Kong, 2002). "The Necessity of Loneliness" was his acceptance speech for the Golden Plate Award at the International Achievement Summit of the American Academy of Achievement, held in Dublin in 2002, and was first published in the Literature Supplement of the Taiwanese daily *Lianhebao* on 11 July 2002. The following essays first appeared in various publications in the early 1990s and were collected in *Without Isms* (Cosmos, Hong Kong, 1996): "Author's Preface to *Without Isms*" (1995), "Without Isms" (1993), "Cold Literature" (1990), "Literature and Metaphysics: About *Soul Mountain*" (1992), "About *Fleeing*" (1991), "The Voice of the Individual" (1993), "Wilted Chrysanthemums" (1992), and "Another Kind of Theatre"

(1993). The remaining essay, "The Modern Chinese Language and Literary Creation" (1996), is from Gao's collection *The Case for Literature* (Ming Pao, Hong Kong, 2001).

An earlier English translation of "The Voice of the Individual" by Lena Aspfors and Torbjörn Lodén was published in *The Stockholm Journal of East Asian Studies* 6 (1995), and an earlier English translation of "Without Isms" by Winnie Lau, Deborah Sauviat and Martin Williams was published in *The Journal of the Oriental Society of Australia* 27–28 (1995–1996).

For this present English-language collection, Gao Xingjian has revised some of his essays, and I have revised my previous translations of "Cold Literature", "The Case for Literature" and "Author's Preface to *Without Isms*", which were included in the Chinese–English bilingual edition of Gao Xingjian, *Cold Literature: Selected Works by Gao Xingjian* (Chinese University Press, Hong Kong, 2005).

"Another Kind of Theatre" demonstrates how far Gao's long-term project to integrate elements of Eastern and Western theatre has advanced over the course of his career. The essays "Author's Preface to *Without Isms*", "Without Isms", "Cold Literature", "About *Fleeing*", "The Voice of the Individual" and "The Necessity for Loneliness" are statements about Gao's views on literary creation, and his belief in the need for the writer to stand apart from collective movements, whether they be engineered by political parties or driven by market or other forces that have nothing to do with literature. In "Literature and Metaphysics: About *Soul Mountain*" he reflects on Chinese and Western narrative techniques, his quest for a narrative style that would allow him to articulate the thoughts that he wanted to express, and his conception of literature. "The Modern Chinese Language and Literary Creation" identifies problems that have arisen in the modern Chinese language since the May Fourth Movement, and details the specific strategies Gao has employed in his determined effort to expand the expressive potential of the Chinese language in his fiction and plays. In his Nobel Lecture and Nobel Centennial Lecture, Gao posits that literature is the most important of human intellectual endeavours because it is capable of revealing many truths about human thinking and behaviour. He argues the case for witness literature, literature that is not bound to promoting any cause, or catering to the dictates of fashion or the market and thus becoming hostage to the dynamics of self-promotion.

In summary, the essays contained in *The Case for Literature* demonstrate the intellectual and aesthetic dimensions of the thinking that informs Gao's creative writings.

Mabel Lee
University of Sydney
July 2006

the case for literature

Author's Preface to *Without Isms*

18 July 1995, France

IN WHAT I CALL "WITHOUT ISMS", "without" may be treated as the verb, that is, "to be without", and "isms" as the noun: "to be without the noun". It may be thought of as a verb–object construction, or even shortened to "no isms". However, if "without isms" is interpreted as a noun it could be inappropriately misconstrued as an ism, such as nihilism.

The premise of "without isms" is "being without"; it is not premised on a void, because then there would be no premise, of course no conclusion, and not even any isms.

In being without isms one is not rashly attempting to establish some sort of theory, but this is not the same as not speaking. Yet there is no beginning and no end; it is speaking for the sake of speaking and does not lead to any conclusions.

To be without isms is not to be without opinions, standpoints or thoughts. But these opinions, standpoints and thoughts do not require verification or a conclusion and do not constitute a system; they end as soon as they are voiced, and they are voiced even if it is futile to voice them. Unless one is physically incapable of speech, if one lives in the world one inevitably speaks. Without isms is in fact simply speech without outcomes.

To be without isms is to some extent more positive than being a nihilist, because there is at least an attitude towards events, other people and the self. Yet this attitude is one of refusing to acknowledge the existence of irrefutable *a priori* knowledge. It may be regarded as a form of rationality — although where this leads does not concern us here — but it is at least not blindly and superstitiously believing in religion or power, and not feeling any need to follow some authority, trend or fashion and thus being led by the nose; nor is it allowing oneself to be shackled to an ideology and thus constructing a prison around one's own feet. There is an amount of individual independence, but of course that independence does have limitations.

Without isms does not treat being sceptical as an ism — that is, it does not treat being sceptical as absolute but instead retains standards of value and behaviour that have been confirmed by the individual. They are values or ethical standards obtained through the individual's own lived experiences, not what has been expounded by others. To negate is also not an absolute logic; indeed, the fact that logical deduction has resulted in absurdities has been empirically proven time and again.

Without isms is not empiricism but does esteem experience. Nonetheless, it does not regard direct experience as the only criterion of knowledge; what has been verified by the experiences of others can also be used to shape one's own judgment. Moreover, experience is not necessarily reliable, nor can it be repeated. Each experience and the next are similarly unique, so there is no need to revere as gospel the experiences of others or even one's own. What is important is that it is the individual's judgment, but it is not necessary to prove whether that judgment is right or wrong. If everything in life had to be verified, there would no longer be any point in living, nor would it be possible to go on living.

As without isms is not an ism, it does not depend upon philosophical speculation or scientific methodology. It is merely a form of understanding, and the task of verifying it can be left to those who are fond of verifying things. Whether human existence is verified or not, people must go on living, and moreover people will go on living just as before.

The starting point of without isms is not to verify, and it is unlikely that a better starting point can be found; a starting point without prior limitations is invariably superior to harnessing yourself to someone else's horse and buggy and letting someone else make you run.

Without isms could be called a choice. Everyone makes different choices, and it is simply one among many choices that you make. You do not force your choice upon others and do not allow others to force their choices upon you.

While without isms affirms that it is the individual who makes the choice, it does not thereby make the individual supreme. Today it is impossible for the individual to be supreme, unless he is insane and believes this to be the case. That romantic sentiment was only a dream. Since the individual cannot control the world, it would be best for him to stand to the side rather than rashly think he can dominate the world. At the same time, there is no need for him to let himself be senselessly butchered by the world. Therefore to be without isms differs from isms that take the individual as the axis, or philosophies that use this as their starting point.

An individual without isms is more human, and for an individual not to be committed to some ism is more in accordance with human nature. Pronouncements on good and bad, right and wrong, virtue and evil may all be set aside, because these are all judgments made by others in accordance with their own sets of criteria. And these judgments all differ because they are derived from different sets of criteria.

Without isms is not individualism. It is not based solely on the judgments of the individual. As far as other people are concerned, every individual is another person, so the judgments and experiences of the individual are only of relative significance and do not possess absolute value.

Without isms is not relativism, but it does use the individual as the starting point, and in making judgments it does refer to self-affirming values. Thus there are inevitably criteria for selection or rejection, although there is no ultimate meaning attached to selection or rejection.

However, without isms involves a choice: between doing something and not doing something. If the choice is to do it, then do it, but the choice not to do something does not mean that one should totally destroy it. If the choice is to do it, then it is best to go ahead and do it to the extent that one can. But there is no need to persist to the point of dying for it, either by letting oneself be killed or by committing suicide.

Therefore without isms is neither nihilism nor eclecticism; nor is it egotism or solipsism. It opposes totalitarian dictatorship but also opposes the inflation of the self to the status of God or Superman. It also hates seeing other people trampled on like dog shit.

Without isms detests politics and does not take part in politics, but is not opposed to other people who take part in politics. If people want to get involved in politics, let them go right ahead. What without isms opposes is the foisting of a particular brand of politics onto the individual by means of abstract collective names such as "the people", "the race" or "the nation".

Without isms does not dream about some imaginary society or social ideal. Such utopias have been destroyed one at a time by reality, and there is no need to fabricate yet another lie about tomorrow.

Without isms does not need to recruit for a group or a faction, or to form an organisation or become a force. It is not a flag bearer or a foot soldier, does not use others and is not used by others.

Without isms does not promote political messages and lacks this capability, but it is not without political attitudes.

Without isms is not anarchism and is not totally opposed to government. Today it is essential for effective government, otherwise society would be a paradise for thugs, terrorists and secret religious sects. There would be no security of property and life, and to talk about being with or without isms would be pointless.

In order to win the freedom of being without isms, dictatorships must be opposed whatever flag they uphold, be it the flag of fascism, communism, nationalism, racism or religious fundamentalism.

To be without isms is the minimum right of a human being. Putting aside any greater freedom, one should at least have that small freedom of not being a slave to any ism.

Without isms opposes profiteering, preaching and indoctrination, but it is not opposed to non-coercive education.

The individual's most rudimentary freedom today is to be without isms. Without this modicum of freedom, can a person still be human? Before discussing this or that ism, people must be allowed to be without isms.

Without isms is a means of protecting the self, and without this prerequisite, raving on about any ism is empty prattle.

However, without isms is not easily achieved. One risks mass public condemnation, even if one avoids being covered in blood as one's head rolls off. In any case, it does not come without a cost. People are born without isms, but after birth various types of isms are foisted upon them, so that if they try to get rid of them later it is not a simple matter. People can change from one sort of ism to another, but they are not permitted to be without isms. The world is strange like this.

Without isms is gained through hard work. I do not use the word "struggle", because struggle is always for an ism and never for the absence of isms. Without isms must initially arise from an awareness in the individual that to be one's own master one must first cleanse oneself of other people's isms. The excision of isms that one has unknowingly consumed, or has been force-fed, is a painful process that can result in psychological trauma, but when one realises that the psychological trauma has been created by others, the trauma and pain will cease and one will be without isms.

To be without isms is a great liberation. Intellectual freedom means not being shackled by isms and thus being able to roam the cosmos like the Heavenly Horse, to come and to go as one will. Saying that customs exist means they exist, and saying they do not means they cease to exist; thus, by saying that customs exist one establishes them, and by saying they do not one liberates oneself from them.

Without isms is closer to the truth, because it is better to seek truth oneself than to look for it by following the road signs on a winding path established by others. As no one has ever found any cast-iron truths, surely it is futile to follow their tracks. Furthermore, since anyone can say that he embraces the truth, clearly there is a plethora of truths, although which brand is closest to the truth remains a problem. So it is best to search for truth oneself.

To be without isms does not preclude the existence of truth, nor, of course, does it confirm the existence of truth. As to whether truth exists or not, if one takes a step back to comment it may not really be taking a step backward — it may even be taking a step forward. But let us not concern ourselves with whether it is taking a step forward or a step backward. Since one is without isms one does not concern oneself with the existence or nonexistence of truth. Moreover, truth could well be a captive bird that once held in the hand will die.

The question of whether or not rules exist in the world depends on how these rules are defined, because the rules of one place may not apply in another place. Universal rules are the same as no rules, so they are not necessarily useful. If there are no universal laws, there will be no universal truth, and there will be no isms.

Without isms is not pragmatism. The self that does not have a market value is not necessarily utterly worthless, because when people are turned into commodities or merchandise it is the very end for them as human beings. If a person cannot say no to being treated as merchandise, and at least preserve this modicum of dignity, will he or she still count as being human?

If the individual is able to say no to power, custom, superstition, reality, other people and the thinking of other people, and to being treated as merchandise, this is probably the last bit of meaning in being human — that is, if existence still has meaning. This, then, is to be without isms.

Without isms does not futilely strive to construct a self-validating system. This is because speculation and dialectics, logic and paradox, and even language, which is the medium for expressing thought, are all highly questionable. Human existence is simply an unsolvable mystery.

Without isms is merely a form of resistance against death by a life that is full of vitality. While it cannot change one's situation, it is at least a gesture, and artistic creation is a trace left by this gesture. Of course, there can also be many other traces, but these are for the individual to choose.

It is a matter of individual choice whether an artist will be with or without isms. In my case, I choose to be without isms.

To be without isms is not to be without reverence, but it is not reverence for spiritual beings, might or death. It is reverence for the boundless unknowable that lies beyond the dividing line of death.

Without isms seems to be pessimistic, but is not pessimism. It is stopping before the brink of despair to look silently around. To know that one is without isms means that one does not need to be afraid or keep searching for something to rely on, and so one is sublimely at ease. This is because to be without isms, one is indeed without isms.

The Case for Literature

2000 Nobel Lecture delivered in December 2000
at The Swedish Academy, Stockholm

I HAVE NO WAY OF KNOWING whether it was fate that has pushed me onto this dais, but as various lucky coincidences have created this opportunity, I may as well call it fate. Putting aside discussion of the existence or nonexistence of God, I would like to say that despite my being an atheist I have always shown reverence for the unknowable.

A person cannot be God, and certainly cannot replace God and rule the world as a Superman. He would only create more chaos and make a greater mess of the world. In the century after Nietzsche, man-made disasters left the blackest records in the history of humankind. Supermen of all types, called "leader of the people", "head of the nation" or "commander of the race", did not baulk at using various violent means to perpetrate crimes that in no way resembled the ravings of a very egotistical philosopher. However, I do not intend to waste this talk about literature by saying too much about politics and history, because I would like to use this opportunity to speak as one writer, in the voice of an individual.

A writer is a normal person — though perhaps a person who is more sensitive than normal, and people who are highly sensitive are often more frail. A writer does not speak as the spokesperson of the people or as the embodiment of righteousness. His voice is inevitably weak, but it is this weak voice that is the most authentic.

What I want to say here is that literature can only be the voice of an individual, and that this has always been so. Once literature is contrived as the hymn of a nation, the flag of a race, the mouthpiece of a political party or the voice of a class or a group, it can be employed as a mighty and all-engulfing tool of propaganda. Such literature loses what is inherent in literature, ceases to be literature, and becomes a substitute for power and profit. In the century just ended, literature confronted precisely this misfortune, and was more deeply scarred by politics and power than in any previous period. The writer too was subjected to an unprecedented degree of oppression.

In order that literature safeguard the reason for its own existence and not become the tool of politics, it must return to the voice of the individual, for literature is primarily derived from the feelings of the individual: one has feelings and articulates them. This is not to say that literature must therefore be divorced from politics, or that it must necessarily be involved in politics. Controversies about literary trends or a writer's political inclinations are serious afflictions that have tormented literature during the past century. Ideology wreaked havoc by turning related controversies over tradition and reform into controversies over what was conservative or revolutionary, thus changing literary issues into a struggle over what was progressive or reactionary. If ideology unites with power and is transformed into a real force, then both literature and the individual will be destroyed.

Chinese literature in the twentieth century was worn out time and again, and indeed almost suffocated, because it was manipulated by politics. The revolution in literature and revolutionary literature alike passed death sentences on literature and the individual. The attack on China's traditional culture in the name of revolution led to the public prohibition and burning of books. Countless writers have been shot, imprisoned, exiled or punished with hard labour over the past hundred years. Such measures were carried to greater extremes than during any imperial dynasty in China's history, and created enormous difficulties for writings in the Chinese language and even more difficulties for discussions about creative freedom.

If the writer sought to win intellectual freedom, he could either fall silent or flee. Because the writer relies on language, not to speak for a prolonged period is the same as committing suicide. If he sought to avoid committing suicide or being silenced, and to express himself in his own voice, he had no option but to go into exile. Surveying the history of literature in both the East and the West, this has always been so: from Qu Yuan to Dante, Joyce, Thomas Mann, Solzhenitsyn and the large numbers of Chinese intellectuals who went into exile after the Tiananmen Massacre in 1989. This is the inevitable fate of the poet or writer who sets out to preserve his own voice.

During the years when Mao Zedong implemented total dictatorship, even fleeing was not an option. The monasteries on faraway mountains that had provided refuge for scholars in feudal times were totally ravaged, and to write even in secret was to risk one's life. To maintain one's intellectual autonomy one could only talk to oneself, and it had to be in utmost secrecy. I should mention that it was only during this period, when literature became utterly impossible, that I came to comprehend why it was so essential. Literature allows a person to preserve a human consciousness.

It can be said that talking to oneself is the starting point of literature and that using language to communicate is secondary. A person pours his feelings and thoughts into language, which, written as words, becomes literature. At the time there is no thought of utility or that some day it might be published, yet there is a compulsion to write because of the reward and consolation to be found in the pleasure of writing. I began writing my novel *Soul Mountain* to dispel my inner loneliness at the very time when works I had written with rigorous self-censorship had been banned. *Soul Mountain* was written for myself, without the hope that it would ever be published.

From my experience as a writer, I can say that literature is inherently man's affirmation of his own self-worth, and that this is validated during the process of writing; literature is born primarily of the writer's need for self-fulfilment. Whether a work has any impact on society only becomes apparent after it has been completed, and that impact is certainly not determined by the wishes of the writer.

In the history of literature there is a large number of great and enduring works that were not published in the lifetimes of their authors. If these authors had not achieved self-affirmation while writing, how could they have continued to write? As in the case of Shakespeare, even now it is difficult to ascertain details of the lives of the four geniuses who wrote China's greatest novels, *Journey to the West*, *Water Margin*, *Jin Ping Mei* and *Dream of Red Mansions*. All that remains is an autobiographical essay by Shi Nai'an, the author of *Water Margin*. Had he not, as he says, consoled himself by writing, how could he have been so totally committed to writing that huge work for which he received no recompense during his life? And was this not also the case with Kafka, who pioneered modern fiction, and with Fernando Pessoa, who was the most profound poet of the twentieth century? Their turning to language was not a quest to reform the world, and despite being profoundly aware of their helplessness as individuals, they spoke out — for such is the magic of language.

Language is the ultimate crystallisation of human civilisation. It is intricate, difficult to grasp, penetrating and pervasive, probing human perceptions and linking man, the perceiving subject, with his understanding of the world. The written word is magical because it allows communication between individuals, even if they are from different races and different times. The shared present time of the writing and reading of a literary work is the reason for the work's eternal spiritual value.

In my view, it is problematic for a writer of the present to try to emphasise a national culture. Because I was born in China and I write in the Chinese language, the cultural traditions of China naturally reside within me. Culture and language are always closely related, and this is how characteristic and relatively stable modes of perception, thought and articulation are formed. However, a writer's creativity begins precisely with what has already been articulated in his language and addresses what has not been adequately articulated in that language. As a creator of linguistic art there is no need to apply to oneself an easily recognisable national label.

Literature transcends national boundaries — and through translation it transcends languages, as well as specific social customs and interhuman relationships created by geographical location and history — to make profound revelations about the universality of human nature. Furthermore, the writer today receives cultural influences from outside his own race, so unless it is to promote tourism, emphasising the cultural features of a people is inevitably suspect.

Literature transcends ideologies, national boundaries and racial consciousness in the same way that the individual's existence basically transcends this or that ism. This is because man's existential condition is superior to any theories or speculations about life. Literature is a universal observation on the dilemmas of human existence and nothing is taboo. Restrictions on literature are always externally imposed, by politics, society, ethics and customs, which set out to tailor literature into decorations for their various agendas.

Literature is neither an embellishment for authority nor a socially fashionable item, because it has its own criterion of merit: its aesthetic quality. An aesthetic intricately related to human emotions is the only indispensable criterion for a literary work. Of course, such judgments will differ from person to person, as they spring from the emotions of different individuals. Nonetheless, such subjective aesthetic judgments do have universally recognised standards. The capacity for critical appreciation nurtured by literature allows the reader also to experience the poetry and the beauty, the sublime and the ridiculous, the sorrow and the absurdity, and the humour and the irony that the author has infused into his work.

Poetry does not derive simply from expressing emotions, although in the early stages of one's writing it is hard to escape unbridled egotism, which is a form of infantilism. There are numerous levels of emotional expression, and to reach higher levels requires cold detachment. Poetry is concealed in the distanced gaze. If this gaze also examines the person of the author and overarches both the characters of the book and the author to become the author's third eye, one that is as neutral as possible, the disasters and the trash of the human world will all be worthy of scrutiny. Then, as feelings of pain, hatred and abhorrence are aroused, so too are feelings of concern for and love of life.

An aesthetic based on human emotions does not become outdated even with the perennial changing of fashions in literature and the arts. In contrast, literary evaluations that fluctuate like fashions are premised on what is the latest — that is, whatever is new is good. This is a mechanism in general market movements, and the book market is not exempt, but if the writer's aesthetic judgment follows market movements it will mean the death of literature. Especially in the consumerist society of the present, I think one must resort to cold literature.

Ten years ago, on completing my novel *Soul Mountain* after seven years, I wrote a short essay proposing this type of literature:

Literature basically has nothing to do with politics, but is purely a matter for the individual. It is the gratification of the intellect, together with an observation, a review of experiences, reminiscences and feelings, or the portrayal of a state of mind ...

The so-called writer is nothing more than an individual speaking or writing, and whether he is listened to or read is for others to choose. The writer is not a hero acting on the orders of the people, nor is he worthy of worship as an idol, but he is certainly not a criminal or an enemy of the people. At times he and his writings will encounter problems simply because of the needs of others. When the authorities need to manufacture a few enemies to divert people's attention, writers become sacrifices. Worse still, writers who have been duped actually think it is a great honour to be sacrificed.

In fact the relationship between the author and the reader — between one person and another person, or a certain number of persons — is always one of spiritual communication through written works; there is no need to meet or socially interact ...

Literature remains an indispensable human activity, in which the reader and the writer are engaged of their own volition. Hence, literature has no duty to the masses ...

This sort of literature, which has recovered its innate character ... can be called "cold literature" ... It exists simply because humankind seeks an entirely spiritual activity beyond the gratification of material desires.

This sort of literature of course did not just come into being today. Yet whereas in the past it mainly had to fight oppressive political forces and social customs, today it also has to do battle with the subversive commercial values of consumerist society. Its existence depends on the writer's willingness to endure loneliness.

... If a writer devotes himself to this sort of writing, he will clearly find it difficult to make a living and will need to seek some other means of livelihood. So the writing of this sort of literature must be considered a luxury, a form of pure spiritual pleasure ...

If cold literature has the good fortune to be published and circulated, that will be due solely to the efforts of the writer and his friends. Cao Xueqin and Kafka are examples of this. Their writings were not published in their lifetimes, so they cannot be said to have created any literary movements or become celebrities. They lived mostly on the margins and seams of society, devoting themselves to this sort of spiritual activity, for which at the time they neither hoped for recompense nor sought social approval. They simply derived joy from writing.

... Cold literature entails fleeing in order to survive; it is literature that refuses to be strangled by society in its quest for spiritual salvation ... If a race cannot accommodate this non-utilitarian sort of literature it is not merely a misfortune for the writer but also a tragedy for that race.

It is my good fortune to have received this great honour from The Swedish Academy during my lifetime, and this is due to the help of many friends from all over the world. For years they have translated, published, performed and evaluated my writings, without thought of reward, and not without difficulties. However, I shall not thank them one by one, for it is a very long list of names.

I would like to thank France for accepting me. In France, where literature and the arts are revered, I have won the conditions for writing with freedom, and I have readers and audiences. Fortunately I am not lonely, although writing, to which I have committed myself, is a solitary affair.

What I would also like to say here is that life is not a celebration, and that the rest of the world is not peaceful as it is in Sweden, where there has been no war for one hundred and eighty years. This new century will not be immune to catastrophes simply because there were so many in the past century, because memories are not inherited like genes. Humans have minds, but they are not intelligent enough to learn from the past, and when evil is ignited in the human mind it can endanger human survival itself.

The human species does not necessarily move in stages from progress to progress, and judging by the history of human civilisation, history and civilisation do not advance in tandem. From the stagnation of medieval Europe to the decline and chaos on the mainland of Asia in recent times, as well as the catastrophes of the two World Wars in the twentieth century, methods for killing people have become increasingly sophisticated. Scientific and technological progress certainly has not made humankind more civilised.

Using some scientific ism to explain history or interpreting it with a historical perspective based on pseudo-dialectics has failed to clarify human behaviour. Now that the utopian fervour and continual revolutions of the past century have crumbled to dust, there is an inevitable feeling of bitterness amongst the survivors.

The denial of a denial does not necessarily result in an affirmation. Revolution did not bring about innovations simply because the new utopian world was premised on the destruction of the old. This theory of social revolution was similarly applied to literature, and turned what had once been a realm of creativity into a battlefield, in which one's predecessors were overthrown and cultural traditions were trampled upon. Everything had to start from zero, modernisation was good, and the history of literature was seen as one of continuing upheaval.

The writer cannot fill the role of the Creator, so there is no need for him to inflate his ego by thinking that he is God. This will not only bring about psychological dysfunction and turn him into a madman but will also transform the world into a hallucination in which everything external to his own body is purgatory, and naturally he will not be able to go on living. Other people clearly represent hell; presumably it is like this when the self loses control. Needless to say, the writer will then sacrifice himself for the sake of the future and expect others to follow suit.

There is no point in rushing to write a conclusion to the history of the twentieth century. If the world sinks again into the tomb of some ideological paradigm it will have been a waste of time, and in any case, people are sure to revise it for themselves later on.

The writer is not a prophet. What is important is to live in the present, to stop being hoodwinked, to cast off delusions, to look clearly at this moment of time, and at the same time to scrutinise one's self. While questioning the world and others, one may as well look back at one's self; this self, too, is total chaos. Disaster and oppression do usually come from a source external to oneself, but man's cowardice and anxiety often intensify his own sufferings and, furthermore, create misfortunes for others.

Such is the inexplicable nature of humankind's behaviour, and man's knowledge of his self is even harder to comprehend. Literature is simply man's focusing of his gaze on his self, and as he does so a consciousness that sheds light on this self begins to emerge.

To subvert is not the aim of literature; its value lies in discovering and revealing what is rarely known, little known or thought to be known, but in fact not very well known, of the truth of the human world. It would seem that truth is the most basic and unassailable quality of literature.

The new century has already arrived. I will not bother about whether it is in fact new, but it would seem that the revolution in literature, revolutionary literature and even ideology have all come to an end. The illusion of a social utopia that enshrouded more than a century has vanished, but when literature throws off the shackles of this and that ism it still has to return to the dilemmas of human existence. These have changed very little and will always be the topic of literature.

This is an age without prophecies and promises, and I think that is a good thing. The writer should also stop playing prophet and judge, since the many prophecies of the past century have all proved to be hoaxes. And there is no need to manufacture new superstitions about the future; it would be much better to wait and see. The writer would do well to revert to the role of witness and simply put effort into presenting the truth.

This is not to say that literature is the same as a document listing facts. There may be facts in documented testimonies, but the reasons and motives behind incidents are often concealed. On the other hand, when literature deals with truth, everything from a person's inner thoughts to the facts of the incident can be exposed without any omissions. This power is inherent in literature as long as the writer sets out to portray the true circumstances of human existence and is not just making up a lot of nonsense.

It is a writer's insights into truth that determine the quality of a work, and word games or writing techniques cannot serve as substitutes. Indeed, there are numerous definitions of truth, and how it is dealt with varies from person to person, but it can be seen at a glance whether a writer is simply embellishing human phenomena or producing a full and honest account. The literary criticism of a certain ideology turned the issue of truth and untruth into semantic analysis, yet such principles and tenets are of little relevance to literary creation.

The question of whether the writer confronts truth is not just one of creative methodology, but is closely linked to his attitude towards writing too. Truth in one's writing also signifies one's sincerity when one is not writing. In this context truth is not simply an evaluation of literature; it has ethical connotations as well. It is not the writer's duty to preach morality, and in striving to portray various people in the world he also unscrupulously exposes himself, including his inner secrets. For the writer, truth in literature approximates ethics, and is the ultimate ethics of literature.

In the hands of a writer with a serious attitude to writing, even literary fabrications are premised on the portrayal of truth in human life, and this has been the vital life force of works that have endured from ancient times to the present. It is precisely for this reason that Greek tragedy and Shakespeare will never become outdated.

Literature is not simply a replica of reality; it penetrates the surface layers and reaches deep into the inner workings of reality. It removes false illusions, looks down from great heights at ordinary happenings and, with a broad perspective, reveals these happenings in their entirety.

Of course, literature also relies on the imagination, but this sort of journey in the mind is not just putting together a whole lot of rubbish. Imagination that is divorced from authentic feelings, and fabrications that are divorced from life experiences, can only end up insipid and weak. Works that fail to convince the author will not be able to move readers. Literature does not rely only on the experiences of ordinary life, nor is the writer restricted to things he has personally experienced. It is possible for what one has heard or seen via some language medium, and what has been related in the literary works of earlier writers, all to be transformed into one's own feelings. This too is part of the magic of the language of literature.

As with a curse or a blessing, language has the power to stir body and mind. The art of language lies in the presenter's ability to convey his feelings to others. It is not some sign system or semantic arrangement that requires nothing more than grammatical structures. If the living person behind language is forgotten, semantic expositions easily turn into games of the intellect.

Language is not merely concepts and the carriers of concepts. Language simultaneously activates the feelings and the senses, and this is why signs and signals cannot replace the language of living people: the intentions, motives, tones and emotions behind what someone says cannot be fully expressed by semantics and rhetoric alone. The connotations of the language of literature must be voiced, spoken by living people, in order to be fully expressed. So as well as serving as a vehicle for thought, literature must appeal to the auditory senses. The human need for language is not simply a need for the transmission of meaning; language is also needed for one to listen to, and for affirming one's own existence.

Borrowing from Descartes, it could be said of the writer: "I say, therefore I am." However, the "I" of the writer can be the writer himself, or be equated with the narrator, or become a character of a work. As the narrator–subject can also be "he" or "you", it can be divided into three. The fixing of a key-speaker pronoun is the starting point for portraying perceptions, and from this various narrative patterns can take shape. It is during the process of searching for his own narrative method that the writer gives concrete form to his perceptions.

In my fiction I use pronouns instead of the usual characters. I employ the pronouns "I", "you" and "he" to talk about or focus on the protagonist. The depiction of one character using different pronouns creates a sense of distance from the character. It also provides actors on a stage with a broader psychological space, so I have introduced changing pronouns into my drama too.

The writing of fiction and drama has not and will not come to an end, and there is no substance to flippant pronouncements about the death of certain genres of literary art.

Born at the start of human civilisation, language, like life, is full of wonders, and its expressive capacity is limitless. It is the task of the writer to discover and develop the latent potential in language. The writer is not the Creator, and he cannot eradicate the world even if he thinks it is too old. Nor can he establish some new ideal world even if he finds the present world absurd and beyond human comprehension. Nonetheless, he can certainly make innovative statements by adding to what other people have said or starting where other people have stopped.

Subverting literature was Cultural Revolution rhetoric. Literature did not die and writers were not destroyed. Every writer has his place on the bookshelf, and he has life as long as he has readers. There is no greater consolation for a writer than to be able to leave a book in humankind's vast treasury of literature that will continue to be read in the future.

Literature is only actualised and of interest at those moments in time when the writer writes it and the reader reads it. If one writes for the future, one is either putting on an act or deluding oneself and others. Literature is for the living and is an affirmation of the present reality of the living. The eternal present and the affirmation of individual life constitute the absolute reason why literature is literature — if one insists on seeking a reason for this huge thing that exists of itself.

When writing is not a livelihood, or when one is so engrossed in writing that one forgets why one is writing and for whom one is writing, it becomes a necessity and one will write compulsively and give birth to literature. This non-utilitarian aspect is fundamental to literature. That the writing of literature has become a profession is an ugly outcome of the division of labour in modern society, and a very bitter fruit for the writer.

This is especially the case in the present age, when the market economy has become pervasive and books have likewise become commodities. There are huge undiscriminating markets everywhere. Not just individual writers but even the literary groups and movements of the past are floundering. If the writer does not bend to market pressures and refuses to stoop to the manufacturing of cultural products by writing to satisfy fashions and trends, then he must make a living by some other means. Literature is not a bestselling book or one on a ranked list, and authors promoted on television are engaged in advertising rather than writing. Freedom in writing is not conferred and cannot be purchased, but comes from a need within the writer himself.

Instead of saying that Buddha is in the heart, it would be better to say that freedom is in the heart, and it simply depends on whether one makes use of it. If one exchanges freedom for something else, then the bird that is freedom will fly off, for this is the cost of freedom.

The writer writes what he wants without concern for recompense not only to affirm his self but also to challenge society. This challenge is not pretence, and the writer has no need to inflate his ego by becoming a hero or a fighter. Heroes and fighters struggle to accomplish some great work or to perform some meritorious deed, and these lie beyond the scope of literary works. If a writer wants to challenge society it must be through language, relying on the characters and incidents of his works, otherwise he can only harm literature. Literature is not angry shouting and cannot turn an individual's indignation into accusations. It is only when the feelings of the writer as an individual are communicated through his work that these feelings will withstand the ravages of time and live on into the future.

Therefore it is actually not the writer who challenges society but rather his works. An enduring work will of course be a powerful response to the times and society in which the writer lives. The clamour of the writer and his actions may have vanished, but as long as there are readers his voice continues to reverberate through his writings.

Indeed, such a challenge cannot transform society; it is merely a very inconspicuous stance taken by an individual who aspires to transcend the limitations of the social ecology. Yet it is by no means an ordinary stance, because it is one that takes pride in humanity. It would be sad if human history were only manipulated by unknowable laws and moved blindly with the current so that the voices of individuals could not be heard. It is in this sense that literature fills in the gaps of history. When the great laws of history are not employed to explain humankind, it will be possible for people to leave behind their own voices. History is not all that humankind possesses; there is also the legacy of literature. Although they are fabrications, the people who appear in literature retain an essential belief in their own self-worth.

Honourable members of The Swedish Academy, I thank you for awarding this Nobel Prize to literature — to literature that is unwavering in its independence, that avoids neither human suffering nor political oppression, and that furthermore does not serve politics. I thank all of you for awarding this most prestigious prize to works that are far removed from the writings of the market, works that have aroused little attention but are actually worth reading. At the same time, I thank the Academy for allowing me to mount this dais to speak before the eyes of the world. A frail individual's weak voice that is hardly worth listening to and that normally would not be heard in the public media has been allowed to address the world. However, I believe that this is precisely the meaning of the Nobel Prize, and I thank everyone for this opportunity to speak.

Literature as Testimony:
The Search for Truth

*Nobel Jubilee Symposium on Witness Literature delivered
in December 2001 at The Swedish Academy, Stockholm*

THE TOPIC I WISH TO DISCUSS is literature and testimony. I am presuming that those here today will not object to the claim that literature testifies to human existence, and would agree that truth is the minimum requirement for such literature. Literature is subservient to nothing but truth, and in this domain of the free spirit, the writer obeys only one command: to search for that truth. In fact, truth has always been the most fundamental criterion of literature — that is, if literature that transcends practical utilitarianism continues to be valued, still justifies personal suffering, and is still worth writing.

However, during the century just ended, politics interfered with and stifled literature to an extent that has seldom been seen in human history. This unprecedented ideological mischief turned literature into political propaganda, or else made it serve political ends. Literary revolution and revolutionary literature did not create a beautiful new world, but instead divested literature of its basic nature, promoted bloodshed, and, by resorting to linguistic violence, turned this domain of spiritual freedom into a battlefield.

Politically engaged literature is widespread both in the West and in the East. Literary criticism is essentially a political judgment that labels writers as leftist or rightist, progressive or conservative. Under authoritarian regimes, these labels are extreme. If a writer is not patriotic, he is a traitor; if he is not a revolutionary, he is a counter-revolutionary — there are no intermediate positions. The tyranny is such that not to have a political attitude is deemed political, silence is protest, and disengagement from politics is simply not allowed.

If literature is to transcend political interference and return to being a testimony of man and his existential predicament, it needs first to break away from ideology. To be without isms is to return to the individual, to return to viewing the world through the eyes of the writer, who relies on his own perceptions and does not act as a spokesman for the people. The people already have rulers and election campaigners speaking in their name.

Of course, the writer who does not involve himself in politics must not flaunt himself as the embodiment of social justice. Needless to say, abstract social justice is not to be found anywhere, and this sort of rhetoric has a very false ring. The writer is not the embodiment of morality either. Short of becoming a sage, how can he instruct the people of the world in morality? And the writer is, of course, not a judge. Oddly enough, while the profession of judge is not at all an enviable one, there are plenty of people aspiring to it. It would be better for the writer to return to being an ordinary person, born in original sin and without special privileges or powers, because this is the most appropriate position from which to observe the human world.

During the century that has just passed, many of the intellectual elite went mad. Following the death of God, it was as if everyone had suddenly become a saviour who wanted to annihilate the obsolete world order or establish a utopia. Naturally some were writers. There is madness in everyone, and intellectuals are not exempted simply because they possess knowledge, since when one loses control over the self, the result is madness.

No one can eliminate self-love, so control of the self is built upon self-observation. Those who possess a certain amount of knowledge, even the very learned, do not necessarily have the capacity for introspection: tyrants and madmen are generally not unintelligent. In fact, human misfortunes are not always due to external pressures, but are sometimes due to people's own weaknesses. The unrestrained bloating of the self distorts the individual's observation of the human world and brings about errors of judgment that can even destroy the individual.

The world did not begin from the self, and it will not come to an end because of a particular individual. The iconoclastic overthrowing of one's predecessors and the eradication of one's entire cultural legacy throughout the twentieth century did not derive solely from a patricidal complex. Linked to the ideology of continuing revolution, it was no longer just an inner impulse but an infectious disease that was able to wreak havoc and bring catastrophe to the world.

If, while observing the boundless universe, the writer is able to scrutinise his own self, and based on this scrutiny of his self also scrutinise others, the incisiveness of his observations will far surpass objective descriptions of reality.

Writers are dissatisfied with purely objective reports on real people and events and instead turn to literature, because through literary techniques they can achieve a deeper understanding of the human world, even though this sort of observation, based as it is only on the individual writer, has its limitations. While subjectivity is inevitable, true human perceptions can be recorded.

It would be best for the writer to revert to being an observer, and to look with dispassionate eyes upon the various facets of human life. If he is able to soberly observe his own self in the same way, he will gain considerable freedom, find the act of observation fascinating, and give up foolishly trying to recreate the world. In any case, a person cannot recreate himself, so he is even less capable of recreating others. This sort of writing has no mission; it is unburdened, does not manufacture falsehoods and can approximate truth.

Literature that does not fabricate lies is written primarily for the writer himself to read. What a person records in a private diary is generally the truth, and it is only if he is anxious that it might be read that he will use a secret code. Yet if the whole diary is in code, and in the end the person cannot decipher it himself, then there is no point in continuing to write the diary.

A writer does not write because he hopes it will provide a livelihood, but because he experiences a real discomfort that needs to be alleviated through writing. This sort of writing does not require pandering to readers, and is in fact the essential purpose of literature.

Unfortunately, the profession of writing becomes more commercialised as a society modernises. Literary products cannot escape market forces and writers must fight to sell their works. This market-driven literature no longer has truth as its main object.

Harassed by continuing political and ideological interference, and squeezed by the escalating cultural commercialisation that comes with economic globalisation, literature that has the truth of human life as its main criterion is forced to retreat to the margins of society. Writers who persevere with this sort of writing can only survive in obscurity, and fortunately this is still possible in the free world. Under autocratic regimes, how can such writers survive without fleeing?

This unfortunate situation in literature actually reflects the existential predicament of human life. Literature that seeks truth refuses to be subservient to politics or to the market, so its readers are limited to people such as those of you here today who are interested in and approve of it. That such readers exist is a good thing in itself, so there should be no need to complain.

This sort of literature is essentially non-utilitarian. Writers who persevere in writing such literature naturally cannot rely on winning prizes, but probably write in the hope of one day gaining recognition. If a writer does not obtain some gratification from this sort of writing it will be hard to sustain, so the search for truth is an indispensable stimulus. The thirst for truth comes with the beginning of life, whereas the ability to lie is gradually acquired during the process of trying to stay alive. However, writers devoted to this type of writing are particularly stubborn. The impulse to search for truth is a passion that demands gratification; it is a form of lust.

Truth has numerous layers, and a simple, superficial statement of facts cannot satisfy the writer. Eyewitness accounts about real people and events, even when not constrained by political or social interdictions, are affected by personal advantage or disadvantage as well as social practice. Their confirmation of truth can therefore only be framed within certain boundaries. A statement in itself predisposes a judgment, because it can only focus on the event itself and cannot deliberate on the causes and consequences. Statements can therefore only remain at the surface layer of fact, and although they satisfy the requirements of the media, they do not reveal deeper layers of truth. Literature as testimony, however, is not satisfied with just a few eyewitness accounts.

It should also be noted that not all eyewitness accounts are reliable. A witness's cowardice or personal standpoint may lead to intentional or non-intentional omissions, and psychological inhibitions may prevent a witness from divulging certain things. And, needless to say, a witness could very well be ignorant of the motives of certain people who may have been responsible for what has taken place. However, literature has no taboos and can transcend all of these problems.

The writer who chooses to write literature as a testimony is, of course, aware that by writing about real people and events or about his personal experiences he inevitably imposes a limitation on his literary creation. But a writer will accept such a limitation, because the search for truth is his overriding goal.

The testimonies of literature are often much more profound than those of history. History inevitably bears the imprint of a ruling power and is therefore revised with each change in power. In contrast, once a literary work is published it cannot be rewritten. This makes the writer's responsibility to history even greater, even if it is not the writer's intention to take on this burden. History can be repeatedly changed because it does not require an individual to take responsibility for it, whereas the writer must confront his own book in print with its indelible black words on white paper.

How much of truth does history conceal? Through retrieving lost memories, the writer seeks the truth that history has concealed, by digging through cold historical materials and, more importantly, making reference to the experiences of living people. Often these are the experiences of the writer himself or his family, so such testimonies naturally have elements of autobiography or biography. When embarking on this sort of writing, it is best for the writer to be an observer in order to maintain adequate distance, especially if dealing with a historical period fraught with disasters. This will allow him to avoid the pitfall of becoming a victim whose writing is bitter and amounts to nothing more than an indictment.

Indeed, this mode of observation can preserve the individual's perspective even if he is confronting immense disasters over a prolonged period. With adequate distance, even if Mount Tai were to crumble he would not be crushed to death. Although his testimony would only be that of one person, it would at least preserve memories overlooked by history and constitute a necessary supplement to history.

Literature that is testimony does not avoid politics — that is, not in content. But it is not political in intent. It does not wave a flag or shout out about any particular line of political action, and certainly does not stand in a war chariot for a particular political faction. It therefore transcends differing political viewpoints. By dealing with taboo issues in the realm of politics, society, religion or social custom, it promotes the uncompromising independence and spiritual freedom that are passionately sought by writers.

A writer can, of course, have a clear political goal, seek to serve in a particular branch of politics, and even join a political party or faction. These choices are for him to make as an individual, providing he does not force others to join him. It is when political involvement is transformed into the unassailable will of the people that all members of society are forced to comply and the whole nation is driven to madness. Under the dictatorship of an authoritarian ruler, this is not uncommon.

The individual should have the freedom to take part or not to take part in politics. But as far as literature is concerned, the writer who engages in politics must be able to disassociate his political engagement from his literary works. Writers from Hugo to Zola and Camus have succeeded in doing so. This very fine tradition among French writers is worthy of emulation in both the East and the West.

In contemporary literature, especially fiction, it has become an increasingly widespread practice for writers to fictionalise their own experiences. By keeping close to what one has been through personally, one's writing is not total fabrication, and it is easier to project oneself into the experience and feel it pulsating with life. However, this is not anything new. Many classics of the past are more or less fictionalised autobiography. From Cao Xueqin to Proust, writers have fused their lived experiences with their inner perceptions, presenting fabrications as real events and concealing real events behind fabrications. As long as authentic human feelings are captured, where is the boundary between fact and fiction? While that boundary may be useful for verifying an author's biography, as far as literature is concerned, it is of no significance. What is of significance is the depth to which human nature is probed and whether or not truth in human life is revealed.

Truth can be reached but cannot be exhausted. Much has already been written about the complexities of humanity and the predicament of survival, but there is still more to be said about life, death, love and lust. Literary revolutions proclaiming the death of antecedents have failed to deliver people from their difficulties. As long as humankind is not completely destroyed by its own madness, literature that probes human life will continue to be written, because more can always be said.

The medium through which humans articulate perception — language — is likewise inexhaustible. Describing an event or an emotion can be an endless quest, and even a momentary impression or a fleeting thought in the inner mind can be related in different ways. Whether or not a description is accurate, as well as fresh, depends on how the narrator views the emotion or event and how he articulates it in writing. The writer is continually searching for a unique narrative method. In other words, he is searching for his own path to articulating what he perceives, even if he has to do this through fabrication.

The writing of fiction of course does not need to adhere rigidly to a particular formula. But it is meaningless to search for a new way of writing unless it is to stimulate clearer perception, just as it is meaningless to explore new modes of literary narration unless this exploration contributes to the search for truth. Stylistic exploration should not be a goal in itself, undertaken for the sake of creating a controversy. Writers have introduced eyewitness accounts, editorial reports, biography, autobiography, memoir, diary writing and even notes into the creation of fiction because they are looking for a path to truth.

Literature's road to truth is built on perceived experiences. The writer relies on his memories of these experiences and on his imagination to evoke new concrete perceptions that act as location markers, giving him access to regions he has not personally visited. Even if what is written is fabrication, it has real perceived experiences as its starting point, and the writer continually returns to these so that his imagination does not become cast adrift or lost in sheer fantasy.

Of course, the writer does not simply depend on the experiences of his own life; he can also draw from the experiences of others. However, such indirect experiences must be able to arouse authentic feelings in the writer before they are introduced into his work, otherwise they will only be so much dead matter. So-called inspiration is direct perception aroused by the stimulation of such indirect experiences; it will suddenly illuminate an inner road leading to truth. While in this state of high concentration, the writer's perception is extremely sharp, and all at once everything becomes so clear that he can almost physically experience even what was previously unknown to him. This sort of awareness is like a scientific discovery and not something the writer is capable of concocting.

Literature can only set out to know human life by using the individual's perceptions as a starting point. Hence it always begins with the perceiving subject, and this predetermines the impossibility of inheriting experience. If the experiences and teachings of others do not pass through the filter of the writer's own lived experiences, they will remain bookish knowledge. Deep-rooted defects within man predetermine that it is impossible for him to change, just as there is no immunisation against jealousy and hostility. This is why mankind will always suffer and go mad, violence and war are inevitable, and lies that are constantly repeated become truth. While education can transmit knowledge, it cannot necessarily awaken the conscience. Literature cannot do this either, and to use literature as a means to educate is merely wishful thinking that both exaggerates the function of literature and restricts its freedom. What can a writer do but leave a testimony of his times?

Perfect beings do not exist. In revolutionary practice, the utopian concept of "new people" deprives men and women of their basic awareness of being human, so that they become tyrants, assassins and hatchet men who can turn a whole country into a prison and a hell. Evil and cowardice are what make people human, and are not proof of God. It would be wiser for the writer to give up trying to be a Creator, a saviour or a Superman, and instead revert to being a frail individual who observes the world and himself.

While scrutinising various facets of human life, the writer may become aware that as an observer he is in fact not so objective, and is at times hindered by prejudice and fanciful thinking. If he also scrutinises his chaotic self, which will usually be in a state of blind self-love, he will naturally become much more sober. He will be released from stubborn bias and delusion and will obtain a greater capacity for scrutiny, which will give rise to feelings of self-deprecation, humour, pity and tolerance. A writer's conscience is an awakening from instinctive chaos and blind violence. This conscience is not innate; it is a pair of clearer eyes that transcends the writer's views of morality and politics, so that what is observed is more profound and more penetrating.

It is the process of writing, not previous training, that allows the writer both to realise these observations of the world with clarity and to transcend his own self. In other words, the writer's self-transcendence is an attitude: he actually turns himself into an observer and sets out not to judge. He sustains this attitude throughout the entire writing process in order to maintain the distance necessary for observation, and his concentration allows for an appreciation of beauty that brings joy, revelation and understanding. This is the reward of the writer who devotes himself to writing that is detached from practical gain. Otherwise it would be difficult for him to sustain such passion while preserving such serenity.

All literature, from ancient times to the present — not only literature that takes real people and historical events as its material — is a testimony to the existential predicament of human life. All writers live in their own times, and the great books in the history of literature are authentic portrayals of their times. In this respect, the myth and the epic profoundly touch upon the truth of human lives. The lyrical poetry that came later on, and the fiction that came later still, also capture authentic human perceptions.

However, history and literature gradually came to be separated, and while the former turned into a record of political authority, the latter increasingly spoke of the true feelings of the individual. Homer's epics of ancient Greece, said to be works controlled by mankind's collective subconscious, were composed before the separation of history and literature. The fiction of Ming and Qing China and of Europe in the nineteenth century tell of various facets of life, based on dispassionate and incisive observations of human relationships in society. Since the advent of modern literature in the twentieth century, concern for the human world has tended to focus on the inner mind; nevertheless, truth remains the fundamental quality of literature.

Other people may be hell, but so too is this totally chaotic self. People whom modernity has turned schizophrenic have also lost their way because of linguistic demons that they themselves have invented. Using words to debunk words as a substitute for truth is the same as using ideology to reform the world. This is the fallacy of people who think that only they are right. Truth is here before one's eyes and does not depend upon speech for description or explanation, and introducing semantic analysis into literature in fact distances it further from truth. Literary theories that employ linguistic concepts can be applied to the literary analysis of a text, but such theories are very remote from literary creation.

To reach truth, one does not have to depend upon metaphysical speculation. Truth is perceptual and concrete. Full of life, truth is available for human observation at any time and in any place; it is the interaction between subject and object. The material world that is external to the subject is the focus of science, whereas literature can only start from an individual's subjective impressions, which affirm truth in human life. To introduce the applied reasoning of science to literature, to turn literary knowledge about people into the construction and deconstruction of concepts, reduces literature to intellectual games and wordplay.

In this age of endless new concepts, any simple idea can be adopted into a certain system and developed into a theory. Even before a theory has been formulated, it can be superseded by a newer concept. Modernism, which initiated changes in literature and the arts at the beginning of the twentieth century, has already succumbed to the dynamics of commodity marketing in postmodern consumerist society. Fashions are continually created yet have no impact on society, and the principle that only the new is good has become meaningless and fails to generate any fresh thinking.

The globalisation of the market economy and the information explosion have left the world of today increasingly bereft of critical thinking. Struggles between political powers have led to uncompromising, antagonistic, bipolar positions that have invaded every corner of social life. The obligation to choose either the left or the right and to be politically correct has replaced independent thinking; if the voice of the writer is not swept into this global chorus, and if he fails to give his allegiance to a political party, he will be marginalised.

Fortunately, literature is a refuge for the free spirit and the last bastion of human dignity. Herein lies the gift of the writer:

when people have turned mute because of their sufferings, he is blessed with a voice.

The language required by literature comes from spontaneous speech that goes straight to truth. Vivid perceptions of a particular instant are without isms and transcend concepts. People are human by virtue of their ability to express themselves in language and to thus become aware of their own existence, not by virtue of their ability to formulate definitions and concepts that explain their existence.

People were people initially without isms; isms were imposed to standardise them. Literary isms, in the same way, force literature into a theoretical framework so that it can easily be embedded in specific ideological or moral teachings that conform with the social and political order.

However, people are still aware of their own humanity because of the unwavering independence of the individual, so there remains a need for self-expression, and for literature. When the old isms come to an end, there is no need to go searching for new ones.

Say goodbye to ideologies and instead return to the truth of being human — that is, return to the true perceptions of the individual, return to this instant, and stop manufacturing lies about tomorrow.

And say goodbye to atrophied historical isms that place aesthetics into chronological sequence and label literature as progressive or conservative, avant-garde or passé, because truly profound works about human life are never passé.

And also say goodbye to the subversion of language. Introducing the strategies of social revolution into literature, or turning literary creation into tumbling word games, in fact removes the human content that is inherent in literature.

Return to human nature, return to focusing on humanity. Such a focus transcends ethical judgments of right and wrong and is superior to all values, because there is no greater value than truth.

However, focusing on humanity transcends all value judgments only if one is able to grasp the pulse of human life. It is the throbbing of life that is supreme. The tremors of frustration, joy, lust and the soul cannot be measured by any system of values.

Observation is superior to and loftier than judgment, because any judgment requires a pre-existing standard. To consider others as hell is to ignore one's own cowardice. Moreover, the reason evil is able to manifest itself is a deficiency within oneself. The distances between serving, giving tacit approval and complicity are not great. If, in the observation of evil, one pays attention to human weaknesses, one will stop making moral accusations, and instead will wonder why evil is able to wreak havoc everywhere and why people are not able to rid themselves of such predicaments.

The greatness of the observer lies in his tolerance. The understanding and compassion that are awakened by observing and reflecting on the human world and on the self far surpass any judgments about injustice or right and wrong. Whether the work is a tragedy or a comedy, if the writer sits in the audience or adopts the position of the reader in order to view his characters, the cleansing and release he experiences will far exceed what he gains from historical testimonies. In the end, the writer is an eyewitness of human nature.

While thus focused on truth, the writer ceases to be concerned with values. To observe and to search for truth thus become the writer's unique and ultimate ethics.

Return to the reality of human life, even if it causes anxiety. When the writer concentrates on truth, he may be able to save the literature that he writes even if he cannot save himself.

Indeed, literature cannot resolve any problems, nor can people resolve those glaringly big rights and wrongs that have no solutions. Can humankind abandon war? Or stop ethnic massacres, political purges, religious fanaticism and terrorism? People cannot prevent man-made disasters — which are millions of times worse than natural disasters — but can only tell of their experiences and feelings about them. In life there is discovery and amazement, perplexity and fear, and of course at times there will be happiness, enthusiasm and excitement, as well as the uncertainty and frustration that breed illusions and fantasies. Literature can only provide a few references for human beings, particularly those who have not seen a great deal of life.

People may not know where they are heading, think they want to go somewhere but cannot get there, or know where they are heading and be striving to get there. But of what significance is this?

If people are somehow affected by literature, moved or awakened, that is enough. If a work can stimulate thinking, then there is a need for it, but if it cannot, then it could very well be dispensed with. When literature arouses feelings and induces thoughts, we should become immersed in these feelings and thoughts and experience their meanings.

At present, readers and writers probably communicate on a similar level. Every individual hopes that others will understand him. But if a minimum understanding between people cannot be achieved, fighting and violence are inevitable, and it is pointless even to talk about tolerance and compassion. For people who are locked into their own experiences, mutual understanding is difficult. Yet through literature there can be a certain degree of communication, so the writing of literature that essentially has no goal does leave people a testimony of survival. And if literature still has some significance, it is probably this.

Without Isms

*15 November 1993, Paris (originally presented as
a paper at the Past Forty Years of Chinese Literature
conference organised by the Taiwanese daily* Lianhebao*)*

I HAVE JUST READ YA XIAN'S "On the Formation of Annual
Rings". He maintains in the essay that it is pointless nowadays
to argue about whether literature is Westernised, traditional or
indigenous. I absolutely agree. Previous to that, there was an
essay by Liu Zaifu called "Goodbye All Gods", in which he
makes the statement that this century's disputes in Chinese
literature have all been fought over foreign issues and have
never jumped out of other people's shadows.

Realism, romanticism, modernism and isms with labels
such as new or old, critical or revolutionary, social or national
or classist were applied to literature, and this heavy burden
made it hard for China's fledgling modern literature to
breathe. Worse still were the numerous isms and definitions of
literary criticism that had insinuated themselves into literature,
so that while banners aplenty could be seen, it was hard to see
any of the works themselves.

Western isms have their own native soils and long histories,
and Lu Xun of course was not wrong to have advocated
importing them; nonetheless his "bring-it-in-ism" was
somewhat excessive. Moreover, is it possible to import
everything? I do not think it is necessary to repeat the road
taken by Western literature. Some isms inevitably will be
imported, but once writers transform these into things of their
own, the original isms will have been considerably distorted,
so it is futile to proceed to verify them and even more futile to
insist on carrying other people's banners.

Literary creation has always amounted to the surging of blood in the writer's own heart, and has nothing to do with any ism. If a work sets out to expound some ism it will certainly die prematurely. Naturally, different writers will have their own literary concepts and artistic methods, but if a writer cannot infuse his works with a life force, then no matter how new the concepts and methods used, his works will sooner or later become passé. I have my own ideas about literature, but I do value artistic form and technique. Western literature — especially many of the concepts and methods of Western modernist literature — has provided me with many insights. However, I do not believe that simply using these concepts and methods will lead to good writing. It is for this reason that I place greater value on the actual works and refuse to stick the label of any ism onto myself.

In 1981 I published that slim booklet of mine, *Preliminary Explorations into the Art of Modern Fiction*, hoping it would open a path for my fiction, which did not conform with China's guidelines at the time. At this point Wang Meng and some other writers published letters that stirred up the "realism versus modernism" debate and resulted in my becoming a modernist. Then in 1983, when a ban was placed on the performance of my play *Bus Stop*, I became an absurdist. In 1985, my play *Wild Man* had a strong flavour of searching for roots because I had discovered a Han folk epic called *Record of Darkness*. Fortunately, Hu Yaobang was in power, so the cultural situation was reasonably liberal and I was not given a label. In 1990, when my play *Fleeing* was published, I was designated a reactionary.

The disaster for Chinese literature is that there must always be judgments to enable the formulation of policies, directions, guidelines, principles, patterns and models, and to determine what is right or wrong, mainstream or non-mainstream. By failing to conform, one is consigned to the ranks of those to be criticised, banned, exterminated, purged, killed or destroyed.

I should say that in both politics and literature I belong to no group, nor am I bound to any ism, including nationalism and patriotism. I certainly have my own views on politics as well as on literature and the arts, but I see no need to nail myself into a certain political or artistic framework. In the present era of ideological collapse and disintegration, if an individual wants to preserve his spiritual independence it would seem that the only attitude he can adopt is to question. I hold this same attitude towards fashions and trends. My experience of mass movements and mass tastes has taught me that these, like the so-called self, need not be worshipped and certainly cannot be superstitiously believed.

As a writer living in exile I can achieve salvation only through literary and artistic creation. This is not at all to say that what I advocate is pure literature, that ivory tower totally divorced from society. Quite the contrary: I regard literary creation as the individual's challenge to society for the right to exist, and although this challenge is insignificant, it is nevertheless a gesture.

Once literature divorces itself from practical gain it achieves enormous freedom. Literature is a luxury that is only possible after issues of survival are resolved, and the fact that people need to enjoy this bit of luxury is something both the writer and the reader can take pride in as human beings. Because of this social aspect of literature, it will always to some extent seek to expose, criticise, challenge, overturn and transcend society.

However, when this social aspect is narrowly confined within the parameters of political function or ethical rules, and literature is turned into political propaganda and moral teachings, or even into an instrument of war for political factions, it is a terrible misfortune for literature. China's literature has not completely freed itself from this. Modern Chinese literature was worn out by political struggles lasting from the end of the previous century to the end of this century, but Chinese writers have now finally escaped from the lair of "literature as a vehicle for the Way", and have the opportunity to speak out as individuals in their own voices.

Literature is essentially an affair for the individual. It can be treated as an individual's profession, but it can also simply express his feelings and dispel his emotions, or it can feign madness so that he can say whatever he wants to gratify his ego, and of course it can also intervene in current politics. What is important is that it is not forced upon others, and naturally it will not tolerate having restrictions imposed upon itself either, whether it be for the sake of the nation or the party, the race or the people. Endowing the will of these abstract collectives with authority can only strangle literature.

For a frail individual, a writer, to confront society alone and utter words in his own voice is, in my view, the essential character of literature, which has changed little from ancient times to the present, whether it be in China or abroad, in the East or in the West. The narrative form used by the writer, his methods and techniques, are secondary. There is a need to say something before there is deliberation on how to say it, and that is the relationship between content and form. Literature requires the need to affirm the existence of the self before art can arise from it.

In the West, a writer's freedom of expression is universally recognised. Nonetheless, from time to time there are instances where writers are oppressed by political authorities. For example, under fascist rule in Germany and Spain, and under communist totalitarianism in the USSR, writers had no choice but to flee into exile. This served to escalate the globalisation of trends in modern Western literary thinking. Released from nation-state consciousness, the writer confronted the world as an individual with responsibility only to the language he used for writing. In this way, the art of language assumed a position of primacy, and how something was said gradually became more important that what was said.

It is for this reason that I have revisited language, although I do not by any means consider the art of language to be literature. It was only after obtaining freedom of expression that I turned my attention to language. Sometimes I even play games with language, but this is not the ultimate objective of my writing. And playing with language is often a trap for the writer. If some meaning that is normally difficult to express is not being conveyed behind the game, it is only an empty language form. I search for new modes of expression because normal language restricts me and does not allow me accurately to express the full extent of my feelings and perceptions. While striving to do so, I gained many insights from Proust and Joyce: their tracking of the conscious and subconscious, as well as constructs they used to achieve different narrative angles. I was also prompted to study differences between the Chinese language and Western languages, and in the process I discovered that syntax in Chinese is not fixed, that the subject and object can be freely transposed, that verbs have neither declension nor tense, that the subject can be dispensed with and that sentences without a pronoun are very common. This being so, all the Chinese grammar books written since *Mr Ma's Comprehensive Grammar*, which have mechanically adopted the rules of Western grammar, should be rewritten. Numerous mechanisms in the structure of the Chinese language can actually trigger off a freer narrative method, and my own method of writing, which I call "flow of language", derives from these.

Pronoun subjects and temporal states in Chinese have fewer restrictions than in Western languages, so there is enormous flexibility when describing the activities of the human consciousness. Chinese is so flexible that short circuits in thinking and semantic confusions often result. In my search for a Chinese language that would more precisely express modern man's rich feelings and perceptions, I wrote novellas and short stories one after the other. It was not until I wrote the story "Buying a Fishing Rod for My Grandfather" that I began to understand that in Chinese reality, memory and imagination are manifested in the eternal present, which transcends grammatical concepts and hence constitutes a time-transcending flow of language. For thoughts and perceptions, consciousness and the subconscious, narration, dialogue and soliloquy, and even the alienated consciousness of the self, I turn to tranquil contemplation rather than adopting the psychological or semantic analysis of Western fiction, and unity is achieved through the linear flow of language. This sort of narrative language has directed the form and structure of my novel *Soul Mountain*.

Incidentally, the research of a young Chinese linguist, Shen Xiaolong, deserves the attention of those who write in Chinese, because a large part of present literary theory is based on Western languages and overlooks the structural characteristics of the Chinese language. The Europeanisation of the Chinese language is so rampant that at times it is unreadable. This problem has existed ever since the new literature movement of the May Fourth period.

The absorption of Western languages into the Chinese language should be distinguished from the Europeanisation of the language. I do not totally oppose the use of Western languages to enrich modern Chinese; I am talking about respecting the language. I try to accord with the linguistic structures that have always existed in the language and not write Chinese that is unintelligible when read aloud. Even when playing with the language to convey content that cannot be expressed in normal sentence structures, I demand of myself that it be pure modern Chinese. At the same time, I do not indulge in computer-like language; after all, I am not a language machine.

Undoubtedly there are aspects of modern Chinese still to be developed, and various writers have made their different contributions. There are also writers who use the spoken language and dialect in their writings, and I think this has enriched modern Chinese. When changing sentence patterns in my search for new modes of expression, I pay attention to the spoken language and dialect. This is important, because if literature in the Chinese language is simply writing to be deciphered and lacks any feeling for the spoken language, it becomes a brain-teasing game for the intellect, or like a rigidly translated novel, and not worth reading. To infuse the spoken language and dialect into the language of literature is also a kind of creation.

Roland Barthes and deconstructionism do not constitute the only direction for the language of modern literature. The French writer Céline, who rescued avant-garde literature through works that used lively spoken language and popular sayings, has provided me with another insight. Modernity in literature does not mean that the style must be burdened with complexities and the writing cannot be read aloud. Moreover, in my view, what constitutes modernity remains problematic. In my novel *Soul Mountain*, and some of my plays, such as *The Other Shore* and *Between Life and Death*, I have put great effort into broadening the expressive potential of the modern Chinese language.

Inevitably, my quest in language at times leads me to doubt its capabilities. Is language in fact able to express people's actual perceptions? My own experience has shown that the harder I try to expand the expressive potential of the language, the further I get from my actual perceptions. The various types of research in contemporary Western linguistics since Wittgenstein have certainly deepened human knowledge about language, but the real world, including man's own existence, lies beyond language. Writing built on semantic analysis has turned literature into an appendage of language, and has nearly brought contemporary literature to a dead end. Hence at times I deliberately destroy language; this can be seen most clearly in my play *Dialogue and Rebuttal.*

The language of Chan Buddhist *gong'an* defies logic and contains meanings beyond the words, which suggested to me that yet another attitude could be adopted towards language. So I vacillate between the two: while attaching a great deal of importance to language, I do not allow it to control me. It would seem that, being infatuated with language, contemporary literature has become lost within its demon walls, and sometimes needs to return to the real world that linguistic analysis has put into parentheses.

Some knowledgable French writers have recently begun to argue for a return to this sort of reality. For the past twenty years Western literature has been undergoing a crisis because it has become lost in linguistic form. Literature loses its life if nonstop changes in form result in a loss of connection with the real world. I attach importance to form, but I attach more importance to reality. This is not limited to external reality, but exists even more vividly in the perceptions of humans living within that external reality. It is in order to articulate and convey this sort of reality that literature resorts to language, even if it is helped by imagination and fabrication.

When writers living in China, Taiwan and Hong Kong, as well as those staying long-term or living in exile in the West, suddenly cast aside, escaped or liberated themselves from the restrictions imposed upon literature and confronted only the Chinese language in which they wrote, they ran into the same problems of linguistic art encountered by Western writers. After charging flamboyantly through the methodologies of modern

Western literature, Chinese literature has entered the flow of contemporary world literature. The current predicament of Western literature also confronts Chinese literature — or to be more precise, Chinese-language literature. Old problems seem to have been resolved, but what are the new problems?

The source of these new problems is to be found in Western literature. It is a fact that during the past century the development of modern Chinese literature has taken place in the shadow of the West, so if Chinese writers want to produce a voice that is different they must understand the path that others have travelled. My interest in modern Western literature has been sparked by a need to provide myself with a frame of reference, so that I would avoid taking a route that others have already followed. Literary creation is interesting precisely because it is the creation of an individual and not replication. It is easy to state this as a principle, but people often live in the shade of others, especially when they truly appreciate certain writers or writings.

My aim has been to try to distance myself from others. Beckett moved from intellectual inquiry to the absurd, but I have repeatedly discovered that there is an element of the absurd in real life. I do not consider the absurd and reality to be in conflict. Beckett endowed the absurd with a sense of tragedy, whereas I prefer to return to comedy. Western avant-garde plays reject realism, whereas my experimental plays are based on real life. Western avant-garde plays resolutely claim to be anti-theatre, but I have retraced Chinese traditional drama to its source and seek to restore what has generally been lost in contemporary drama: theatre and theatricality. Moreover, I strive to find and realise new possibilities for theatre and theatricality in both playwriting and performance methods.

I must admit that modern Western literature has stimulated me more than modern Chinese literature has. Chinese literature from the May Fourth period onwards was constrained by the limitations of China's political and social environment and endlessly embroiled in the various debates foisted upon it, so there was no time to address literary problems. But those debates, which were imposed on literature and had nothing to do with it, now seem to have ended. The fact that today Chinese writers, or to be more precise Chinese-language writers, are able to transcend political and ideological restrictions and meet with one another is to some extent a good sign.

The present age is not a time for reading in isolation, because cultural communication between the East and the West, and indeed between all the various peoples of the world, is no longer too big a problem. A writer who is devoted to writing and has responsibility only for his own written language will strive to absorb and reproduce in his own creations all that interests him in the cultures of humankind, from ancient times to the present.

I believe that there is little difference between Chinese and Western writers in their attitude towards creative writing. Of course, many writers bring with them the profound cultural achievements of their own people, and these will naturally be reflected in their writings, but this is totally different from deliberately sticking on a cultural label to please others in order to promote sales. Living in exile, the Polish writer Gombrowicz was quite right in saying that Poland was there inside himself, and even though at times he uses gimmicks from American detective stories in his writing, the loneliness and cold of Eastern Europe can still be felt. Joyce's *Ulysses* is set in his native land, but no one would read it simply as a novel that describes Irish life. Neither writer ever returned to his homeland.

Living in exile has not been bad for me; instead, it has given me even more points of reference. By completing my novel *Soul Mountain* and my play *Romance of "The Classic of*

Mountains and Seas", I was able to cure my so-called homesickness. The former deals with feelings induced by the social realities of China, and the latter with reflections on the origins of Chinese culture; I spent many years of hard work writing both of these. When a person is suddenly divorced from his ancestral land, a distance is created that allows him to become more detached in writing about it. Chinese culture is already infused in my blood and there is no need for me to stick a label on myself. In my own way I have already sorted out what is positive and what is negative in traditional Chinese culture. It is important for a writer to be able to transcend cultural traditions, and not to depend on selling his ancestral heritage in his work in order to make a living. Writing has always relied on the individual, unlike other occupations, which must rely on the cooperation of various sectors of society, including the government. Conversely, any form of collective will that is imposed on writing can only be disastrous. The writer is neither the representative of his culture nor the spokesperson of his people, and if he has the misfortune to become such a representative or spokesperson he will inevitably no longer be recognisable as a writer.

It might be said that my play *Fleeing*, which I wrote for an American theatre, was inspired by the events in Tiananmen Square. I removed the setting from the historical reality and made it into a political philosophy play without any heroes. The Americans wanted me to make changes, so I withdrew the manuscript and paid for the translation myself. When I write I have my own things to say and I will not make compromises to please the tastes of others. The writer faces society alone and speaks and narrates in the voice of the individual; for me it is this voice that is closest to truth.

There are reasons why literature over the past century has promoted the worship of the self to the extent that the self virtually attained the status of God. However, in retrospect, if one really thinks of oneself as God, even if one escapes going mad like Nietzsche, it will not be easy to escape the fate of idols — falling down and breaking into pieces. Nietzsche went mad and is dead, and Nietzsche-styled selves have now been deconstructed. In this postmodern age, which is concerned only with consumerism, the unchecked bloating of the individual is already a far-off myth that probably had its origins in the narcissism of people's youth. Rather than the starting point of modern literature, Nietzsche's Superman should more accurately be seen as the end point of romanticism. Kafka's self is a more accurate depiction of modern man. After him, a brilliant analysis of the self is to be found in some hundred thousand lines of posthumously published poetry by the Portuguese poet Fernando Pessoa.

The self is of no significance in the world, but it has boundless wealth because human feelings about the boundless universe are ultimately derived from the self. Modern literature is a return to the perceiving subject, and it is through the mirror of the self that the world is reflected. Literary truth is the truth of these perceptions, and the world external to these perceptions is beyond the concerns of literature. In modern literature, the affirmation of the perceiving subject and its replacement of the all-knowing and omnipotent narrator, who is normally the author, has cast aside unquestioning ethical judgments of right and wrong, but the search for self has led to schizophrenia. So, as I see it, the history of twentieth-century literature may be summarised as the replacement of disintegrating traditional values with this sort of modernity. After the discovery of the self at the end of the last century there inevitably came the doubting of the self. Now it is the end of another century.

The fact that evil is not confined to others and one's own self is an eternal hell has intensified the doubting of the self. If I were to sum up my recent play *Nocturnal Wanderer*, I would say that it is about the impossibility of winning the war against evil. There is no trace of anything Chinese in the setting, and its only discernible difference from a play by a Western author is its attitude of tranquil contemplation. This attitude, which I always adopt towards society and the self, can of course be said to derive from entrenched Chinese cultural traditions, and it is quite different from the psychological analysis and traditions of Western writers. Yet the non-action of Daoist philosophy and the renunciation of the world that is central to Buddhism are too negative for me, because I do in fact want to achieve something. I am neither Daoist nor Buddhist, and what I adopt is simply an attitude of observation and scrutiny. The narrative language of my fiction and my so-called tripartite theory of theatre performance are derived from this sort of attitude.

Can a Chinese intellectual living in the West preserve his spiritual independence as an individual without embracing an ism or seeking consolation in Chinese cultural traditions? I have only doubts, and even doubt all notions of value. It is only life that I do not doubt, because I myself am a being who is full of vitality. Life has a significance that is above ethics, and if I have any value it lies in my existence. It is hard for me to contemplate either suicide or the killing of my spirit prior to the arrival of natural death.

For me, literary creation is a means to salvation; it could also be said that it is a means to life. It is for myself, not to please others, that I write. And I do not write to change the world or other people, because I cannot even manage to change myself. For me, what is important is simply the fact that I have spoken and the fact that I have written.

It is now apparent that literature can transcend ideology, and Baudelaire and Dostoevsky have already shown that it transcends ethical judgments. What literature cannot be separated from is aesthetic judgments, and it is the writer who generates tragedy, comedy, poetry, absurdity, farce or humour. Some modern writers have expunged ethical judgments from their writings, but it is impossible to dispense with subjectivity in their aesthetic judgments. This is the last bastion of the writer's authority and is why literature continues to exist.

As a writer I strive to position myself between the East and the West, and as an individual I seek to live at the margins of society. In this era in which, to use Liu Xiaofeng's words, the physical body ridicules the spirit, this is a better choice for me. Yet there is no way of knowing whether or not I will be able to continue doing this.

Cold Literature

30 July 1990, Paris

In my view the time for rousing revolutionary literature has passed, because the revolution has already revolutionised itself to death and has left behind only bitterness and a sort of weariness, listlessness and even nausea.

Literature basically has nothing to do with politics, but is purely a matter for the individual. It is the gratification of the intellect, together with an observation, a review of experiences, reminiscences and feelings, or the portrayal of a state of mind.

Due entirely to political need, literature unfortunately grew fervent, and was subjected to attack or flattery. It was helplessly transformed into an instrument, a weapon or a target, until it finally forgot its basic nature.

The so-called writer is nothing more than an individual speaking or writing, and whether he is listened to or read is for others to choose. The writer is not a hero acting on the orders of the people, nor is he worthy of worship as an idol, but he is certainly not a criminal or an enemy of the people. At times he and his writings will encounter problems simply because of the needs of others. When the authorities need to manufacture a few enemies to divert people's attention, writers become sacrifices. Worse still, writers who have been duped actually think it is a great honour to be sacrificed.

In fact the relationship between the author and the reader — between one person and another person, or a certain number of persons — is always one of spiritual communication through written works; there is no need to meet or socially interact. The writer bears no responsibility to the reader and the reader has no need to make impositions on the writer. It is for the reader to choose whether or not to read a work.

Literature remains an indispensable human activity, in which the reader and the writer are engaged of their own volition. Hence, literature has no duty to the masses or society, and ethical or moral pronouncements added by busybody critics are of no concern to the writer.

This sort of literature, which has recovered its innate character of giving vent to the writer's feelings and telling of his ambitions, can be called "cold literature", to differentiate it from literature that promotes a creed, attacks contemporary politics or tries to change society. Cold literature will of course not be newsworthy and will not arouse public attention. It exists simply because humankind seeks an entirely spiritual activity beyond the gratification of material desires.

This sort of literature of course did not just come into being today. Yet whereas in the past it mainly had to fight oppressive political forces and social customs, today it also has to do battle with the subversive commercial values of consumerist society. Its existence depends on the writer's willingness to endure loneliness.

Indeed, this kind of writer has even more difficulties than other writers. If a writer devotes himself to this sort of writing, he will clearly find it difficult to make a living and will need to seek some other means of livelihood. So the writing of this sort of literature must be considered a luxury, a form of pure spiritual pleasure. No matter how prosperous and vibrant a society, it is a tragedy if it cannot accommodate this sort of spiritual activity by an individual.

History is unperturbed by such tragedies and simply records humankind's activities, or perhaps does not even leave a record of these. If cold literature has the good fortune to be published and circulated, that will be due solely to the efforts of the writer and his friends. Cao Xueqin and Kafka are examples of this. Their writings were not published in their lifetimes, so they cannot be said to have created any literary movements or become celebrities. They lived mostly on the margins and seams of society, devoting themselves to this sort of spiritual activity, for which at the time they neither hoped for recompense nor sought social approval. They simply derived joy from writing.

Exhausted by almost a century of being politically and ethically correct, Chinese literature has now fallen into a morass of isms, ideologies and debates on creative methodology that have little to do with literature but from which it cannot extricate itself. It is only by fleeing from these interminable and unintelligible debates that the writer can save himself. Literary creation is basically a solitary form of work in which no movement or collective can assist; they can only strangle it. It is only by resolving not to become attached to a political group or movement that the writer is able to win complete freedom.

This does not mean that the writer therefore does not have his own political attitudes and ethical viewpoints. When subjected to political and social pressures, writers do have things to say, and it is perfectly all right for them to give speeches and make public statements, but it is important that these are not introduced into their literary creations. I believe that while politics and society may be touched upon in literary creation, the best option is still to flee; it deflects social pressures and also cleanses one spiritually. Therefore, I also think that it is best for the writer to locate himself at the margins of society so that he can quietly observe and reflect, as well as immerse himself fully in cold literature.

The problem is that successive wars, revolutions, political movements and struggles in China over the past hundred years have had an impact upon every level of the country's intellectual world. Dissenting voices have not been tolerated, and writers have been forced to become fighters, otherwise they would not have been able to make a living. They have failed to save either the people or the nation, and have often sacrificed their property and even their lives. Cold literature is possible only if the pressures of politics and society can be escaped and a livelihood guaranteed. This is why it has been difficult for modern Chinese literature to be cold.

It may therefore be said that cold literature entails fleeing in order to survive; it is literature that refuses to be strangled by society in its quest for spiritual salvation. I also believe that if a race cannot accommodate this non-utilitarian sort of literature it is not merely a misfortune for the writer but also an indication of the utter spiritual impoverishment of that race.

Such are my reasons for proposing cold literature.

Literature and Metaphysics: About *Soul Mountain*

May 1991, Stockholm (lecture presented at the East Asian Institute, Stockholm University)

CHINESE IS THE LARGEST language group in the world today in terms of the number of people who speak it, but how much freedom does one have in using it? Firstly, this is a political issue; then there are social pressures that create psychological self-constraints in the writer, and lastly there is the issue of the language itself. The writer confronts only language in his writing, but first he must deal with myriad pressures and seek to transcend them. The writer writing in Chinese often struggles helplessly with these extra burdens, so that by the time he comes to confront the art of language he is already exhausted. One would have to concede that he really has a great deal to contend with.

In 1981, I was encouraged by an enthusiastic friend to publish a slim volume about the art of language for the general reader called *Preliminary Explorations into the Art of Modern Fiction*. I had been finding it hard to publish my fiction and thought that this might open a path for it. I certainly did not imagine that publication would continue to be difficult. I had sent a collection of my short stories to five publishers in China, and finally to a Hong Kong publisher, but all to no avail.

Surprisingly, this small book, which contained not the slightest hint of politics, stirred up a huge debate over modernism versus realism. It created numerous problems for me, and caused trouble for many of my friends, as well as some veteran writers who had shown concern for me, such as Ba Jin, Xia Yan, Ye Junjian, Yan Wenjing and Zhong Dianpei. Worse still, Wang Meng, who had written an open letter to me about my small book, became the target of attacks. This is why it may be said that extravagant talk about the art of language in China is really quite difficult.

In the summer of 1982, a kindly editor of a publishing house, who wanted to know whether the things I had proposed for fiction were actually possible, asked me to write a novel. I immediately agreed, but on the condition that it would be published without anything deleted. That was how *Soul Mountain* came about. I should add that he had no idea how the novel would turn out; he simply trusted me. Later he also gave me an advance royalty of four hundred *yuan* from the publishing house because I told him I had to go on a trip: the campaign to attack me had already been launched. Even as I structured the novel I knew that it could not be published, but to repay this small royalty I intended to submit a handwritten manuscript when the time came. For me that would count as the end of the matter, and I would be free of any psychological burden.

In September of 1989, I finally completed the manuscript in Paris. However, this was soon after the Tiananmen events, and to have sent the manuscript would only have caused the publishing house unnecessary problems, so I decided not to send it.

My writing of the book was in fact helped by the ban imposed on performances of my play *Bus Stop*. If this lyrical comedy on life could be turned into a political issue and be targeted in the Purge Spiritual Pollution Campaign, then surely this novel of several hundred thousand words which I was writing with no taboos would be construed as a serious crime. So I liberated myself from society, people, ethics, and even so-called writer's responsibility and original sin, and proceeded to write freely, confronting only my mother tongue, the enduring Chinese language.

It is my view that the only responsibility a writer has is to the language he writes in. He can reform his creations as much as he wants, talk endlessly, write about nothing and play with the language, but he must respect the rules inherent in the language, otherwise there will be no art of language.

During the vernacular language movement of the May Fourth period, the ancient Chinese language experienced a rebirth that improved its capacity to express modern man's feelings. To a large extent this was due to the significant number of outstanding writers in the history of China's modern literature. However, Mao Zedong, despite being a stylist himself, then turned the Chinese language into something appalling over the long period when he was in power. I believe that what authors who write in the Chinese language today can do together, in addition to their individual undertakings and literary ideas, is develop the potential of the language, so that it will more fully express the feelings of modern people. This was my rationale for writing *Soul Mountain*: I wanted to demonstrate that there was space in the language for greater creativity.

I find Europeanised Chinese intolerable: undiluted Western morphology and syntax are applied to the language so that it becomes unreadable. This started off with some poor-quality translations. Afterwards it was introduced into numerous literary works, and eventually some theorists with no understanding of Western languages began advocating it, wrongly thinking that it was a modern literary style. Defective sentences and writing that was illogical and ungrammatical were treated as the latest trends, and subsequently came to be discussed and annotated. Such theorists are totally ignorant of the fact that while Beckett was concise and Roland Barthes discursive, their recreations of language and their expositions of texts were written in a very pure form of French. The contamination and chaos in the Chinese language created by rebellious language tyrants do not need to be endorsed even if they are an inevitable stage in the struggle for freedom of expression. Now that the Chinese language has undergone that trauma, a fresh form of the language should emerge.

Further investigation of this contamination reveals that it is also the result of a lack of research into the grammar of modern Chinese. When linguists standardised the modern Chinese language, they were largely guided by the grammar of Western languages, and they explained it in terms of morphological and syntactical concepts borrowed from Western languages, while ignoring structural features inherent in the Chinese language. This of course has been useful for teaching Chinese, compiling Chinese-language textbooks for Westerners and proliferating standard Chinese, but it is far removed from the writing of Chinese literature.

The translation of modern Western linguistic and theoretical writings further worsened the crisis in modern Chinese, because research based on Western languages and Western-language literary works was shifted wholesale into Chinese-language writings, and this resulted in a rigid translation genre.

The older generation of linguists of course achieved a great deal in terms of standardising the vernacular language, but in the case of the language of new Chinese writing, linguistic research seems to have stalled. Perhaps I am presumptuous in thinking that if parallels were drawn between ancient Chinese and the present spoken language — without making any reference to the grammar of Western languages — it would be possible to work out a modern Chinese grammar that corresponded more closely with the characteristics of the Chinese language. This could open up another path in modern linguistics, because all existing linguistic theories are based on a few European languages. If translations of Western writings and introductory essays about them are written without reference to the structure of Chinese, it easily leads to the Westernisation of the language. But this sort of research into the Chinese language it seems has yet to begin.

I actually do not object to the introduction of new words and concepts, or even new syntax, from Western languages, but ideally these should be blended into the structures inherent in the Chinese language. When I wrote *Soul Mountain* as part of my search for a modern Chinese language, that was the principle I adopted. I believe that the existing Chinese language cannot adequately represent all the feelings of modern man, but I also believe that it is possible to enrich the existing language. However, to be creative in the language requires first of all that one have a solid grounding in it.

I am not proposing a return to the ancient Chinese language, and in principle I am not in favour of writing that is filled with allusions and long-dead idioms. Even if I occasionally pursue a particular genre, for example in isolated sections of *Soul Mountain*, I avoid lapsing into cliché, because despite their beauty, ancient Chinese expressions ultimately cannot replace the writer's own creations.

It seems that other tendencies are to promote the short essays of the late Ming period and to imitate the writings of Lao She. Both, one must concede, represent exceptionally pure forms of Chinese, but in my view these forms of language are already history. It is fine to write about the city folk of old Peking in the language of Lao She, but when it comes to writing about the young people of present-day Beijing that language is obviously inadequate, and when it comes to describing the psychological activities of modern-day people things become even more difficult.

I advocate writing in the living language. The spoken language of present-day people is fresh and vivid, and a rich source for the language of literature. Oral folk literature, such as comic dialogue, the storytelling and ballad singing of Suzhou, and even folk songs prior to the time when scholars made them conform to five- or seven-word patterns are all examples of primitive oral records of events. I have discovered in these some ingenious word formations and highly complex sentences. For example, the piling up of words and the swinging sentences of folk songs found in the Wu dialect region of Taihu embody many mechanisms that can enhance the expressive potential of Chinese.

I also think that the dialects of each locality contain many words that can express emotions and convey ideas more effectively than is possible in Chinese that has gone through a process of standardisation. For example, much of the vocabulary of the Sichuan dialect is immediately comprehensible to people who are not Sichuanese, and with minimal modification it can be introduced into the language of literature. Used appropriately, the vocabulary, word formations and syntax of some dialects can help enrich the modern Chinese language. A large amount of this kind of experimentation was carried out in *Soul Mountain*.

In searching for my own language, I was enlightened much more by Feng Menglong and Jin Shengtan than by the French surrealist poets. Feng used the living language in his books. The vivid language of *Midnight Songs of the Wu Region*, which he compiled, came from the same source as the recorded folk songs collected by my friend Ma Hanmin, and I marvel at the ingenuity and complexity of Feng's sentences. The great literary critic Jin Shengtan made the dead literary language of books come to life; read aloud, his narrative language resonates, swirls and bends, and his long sentences undulate in a flowing rhythm of great elegance. Both Feng Menglong and Jin Shengtan were masters of language, and their very substantial contributions to Chinese language have no parallel in bureaucratic Confucian writings. Nevertheless, relegated to a volume separate from orthodox Chinese literary history, they share the fate of the great novelists Shi Nai'an, Cao Xueqin and Liu E.

I believe the language of literature should be such that it can be read aloud — that is, the written words must have auditory appeal. Sound is the soul of language, and this is how art in language differs from the academic study of poetry and prose. Even when people whisper or soliloquise at the most primitive level — *nan-nan-na-na* — they cannot divorce themselves from the direct perception of sound. The beauty of Chinese characters is visual, but calligraphy is another form of art. For Westerners who cannot speak Chinese, the images elicited by Chinese characters have a special fascination. This is understandable, but unless the images are linked to the sound, feel and syntax of the language, they are merely a script, not a living language.

Monosyllabic in its basic structure, each word has a vowel and is attributed one of four tones; these are vital to the musicality of the Chinese language. I place importance on the sounds and the rhythms so derived, and my search for a modern Chinese language does not oppose these. This of course has to do with my being fond of using a tape recorder when writing, although I have never treated a recording as the final manuscript and I often make many revisions. Some chapters of *Soul Mountain* were revised more than twenty times. I persevere with using a tape recorder in my writing because it helps elicit a direct perception of the language. Some friends have drawn certain comparisons between *Soul Mountain* and the language of the late French writer Georges Perec. I do not mind such comparisons; after all, Perec was a genius in the art of language.

Sometimes I play with the language, but only to convey sentiments that are hard to express using conventional sentence modes. If I occasionally destroy the rhyme and rhythm of something, it is when I am making fun of it to convey a certain feeling in the language. However, I always respect the basic structure of the Chinese language. I reject the idea of tinkering with some form of computer language, or playing with words and phrases as if they are poker cards.

I should emphasise that my experimentation with language is not aimed at destroying the Chinese language. Nor do I treat a certain dead official writing style as anathema. Since that style is already dead, why should I waste my time thinking about it? Anger in language, or angry language, cannot express my perceptions as a man in the modern world. Whether or not I will ever know what the ultimate meaning of language is does not concern me.

I am not a philosopher. The present age is not one of philosophy, because theory has progressively replaced intellectual inquiry, and traditional philosophy came to an end with Wittgenstein. What I call metaphysics is simply a mode of thinking, and contains none of the ontological questions or implications of philosophy. Nevertheless, in the final analysis both literature and philosophy are expressed in language. My intention here is not to explore whether or not language is capable of discussing everything; I am simply searching for a modern form of Chinese that is capable of fully expressing my perceptions.

I am also not trying to set myself up as a judge who will formulate new patterns of language. Being the subtlest quintessence of human culture, language is a spontaneous entity. Its basic nature is greater than politics, not to mention any particular political power. It is greater than ideology, disregards rules of philosophy or ethics and, to an even greater extent, social customs. Through language, it is possible to transcend oneself and establish one's own controls and rules. This is probably why the art of language — that is, literature — will broach no interference and continues to have an independent existence. I believe this to be the case and am trying to find what I consider to be a pure form of the modern Chinese language with which to plot my own perceptions.

Stream of consciousness in modern Western literature begins with a subject. In delineating and capturing the perceptual processes of this subject, the writer invariably obtains a flow of language. Therefore, this literary language might well be designated as a "flow of language". I further believe that this sort of language can be given even greater expressive power just by changing the angle of perception of the subject, for example by changing the pronoun, using the second-person pronoun "you" instead of the first-person "I". Or, the third-person pronoun "he" could be used instead of "you". By changing the pronoun, the same subject is endowed with different angles of perception.

In *Soul Mountain*, what is related via the three changing pronouns is different perceptions by the same subject, and this encapsulates the linguistic structure of the book. The third-person pronoun "she" is best described as the male subject's experiences and thoughts regarding the other sex, with whom a direct link is impossible. In other words, the book is a long soliloquy in which the pronouns keep changing. I prefer to call this a flow of language.

Language is inherently not concerned with logic. As an expression of the psychological activities of humankind, it simply follows a linear process as it seeks actualisation. Moreover, it does not obey the objective concepts of time and space that belong to the physical world. When the discussion of time and space is imported into linguistic art from scientific aims and research methods, that linguistic art is entirely reduced to trifling pseudo-philosophical issues.

By not indicating tense, the Chinese language better reflects the basic nature of language. Actualised in language, present, past and future are identical and indistinguishable, and are not emphasised by inflecting the verb; only the psychological processes of the narrator and the listener or reader are involved. Moreover, reality and imagination, memory and thought have no strict demarcations but are integrated within the process of the narration, which acknowledges only this actualisation in language and is not concerned with the real world.

Narration should be left to literature, but its analysis can be handed over to scientists. Even if at times it lacks the precision for scientific explanations, the Chinese language is more adept at describing psychological activities than Western languages, which are logical and analytical. Metaphysical linguistic studies and the various types of analytical linguistic studies of today are undoubtedly useful for research on computers and artificial intelligence, but have little meaning for literature. My interest in the potential of language and its power of expression is not academic, but is an attempt to understand and track psychological states. Like art, literature is a place seldom frequented by science. To have different interpretations is precisely what is most wonderful about literature, so if different interpretations result it is not a disaster.

"To be or not to be" is a simple division of one into two, a rudimentary form of philosophy. One divided by three or one divided by infinity is a return to chaos, and such an understanding is loftier. The meaning of language does not lie in the defining of language, but in the process of its actualisation; meaning is what others bestow upon it. Articulation in language is superior to verfication, and much more worthwhile. Moreover, is the verification of language possible?

The word "be" is a peculiar word. "To be or not to be" implies that something can "be" yet can also "not be". To say that the twentieth century is a scientific era and to say it is an era of swindlers are both equally pointless. In all vocabularies it is the word "what" that is most interesting; it can give rise to all sorts of narratives, limitlessly, endlessly.

I have no intention of verifying anything, and I do not need to force some sort of knowledge upon others, nor do I hope that they will accept it. The important thing is that I have spoken.

My relationship with myself has nothing to do with self-worship. The almighty heroes who have replaced God with the self and those who have tragically expunged the self disgust me equally. Apart from myself, I am nothing.

What I experience are merely viewpoints or, one could say, narrative angles. I am a linguistic subject from whom perceptions arise. So my existence simply consists of narrating these perceptions.

In the Chinese language the subject is often omitted and the verb is not inflected according to the pronoun, so the narrative angle can change with great ease. It can shift freely from "I" with a subject to "I" without a subject — in other words, from I, to the deletion of "I", to the nonexistence of "I" — then change to "you", then to "him". "You/I" is the objectivised form of me, and "he/I" may be regarded as me departing from my physical body to quietly contemplate or to observe and reflect, so there is enormous freedom. In writing *Soul Mountain* I discovered this freedom.

Speculation in Western traditional philosophy, that is, metaphysics, originated in Western languages, and such languages may be thought of as analytical. By contrast, the linked-word-order structure of the Chinese language gave rise to a different type of philosophy, also known as metaphysics but based on Daoist and Confucian thinking. The differences between Eastern and Western cultures derive primarily from the differences between these two language systems. In the final analysis, all philosophies are articulated in language, in exactly the same way as literature is.

The two major directions in contemporary Western literature, psychological analysis and semantic analysis, have their origins in the capacity of Western languages to endlessly dissect psychological phenomena or search for the implications of words. This also accounts for the numerous treatises in the West based on phenomenology and analytical philosophy.

Since I write mainly in Chinese, and only occasionally translate, I prefer to find another path. I believe that when the Chinese language has extricated itself from politics and ethical preaching, it will be able to give rise to a modern Chinese literature that is infused with Eastern spirituality. If cultural interactions between the East and the West lead only to the same trends, then while it will be a boisterous world, it will inevitably be rather monotonous.

While seeking to track my feelings in *Soul Mountain* I avoided any static psychological analysis. I resorted only to deep contemplation, so while my thoughts roamed in language, the meanings lay beyond words. I have an aversion to maxims and aphorisms and do not mince words. My efforts in language have been devoted more to fluidity than to meticulous rhetoric, even if they include sentence patterns that I have invented with complex structures. I also strive for sensuousness in language by simply relying on how something sounds, so there is really no need for readers to insist on trying to work out the meaning. In this I should acknowledge the great insights provided to me by *Zhuangzi* and the Chinese translation of the *Diamond Sutra*.

Daoism and Chan Buddhism, in my view, embody the purest spirit of Chinese culture, and they have brilliantly manifested this through their play with language. Being endowed with the perceptions of a person living in the modern age, I propose recapturing this spirit in the modern Chinese language.

I want to write something fresh, not eat the fruit someone else has already been eating. This attitude of wanting new experiences is common to everyone, but does not mean one is trampling on one's predecessors. To overthrow is a meaningless slogan, particularly in the realm of literature and the arts. It is like criticism, and the vicious circle of criticism of criticism has never brought any results. I cannot help being sceptical about that sort of revolutionary progressivism.

I reject the notion that innovation demands the negation of tradition. Tradition exists, and it is simply a matter of how one understands or makes use of it. Whether one makes use of it or not is for the individual to decide and there is no need to argue about it. For me, using tradition to attack people and denigrating tradition are both reprehensible.

I appreciate China's old traditions in fiction, and I revere the writers Pu Songling, Shi Nai'an, Cao Xueqin and Liu E. I also appreciate Tolstoy, Chekhov, Proust, Kafka, Joyce and some French *nouveau roman* writings. However, while I have gained much from all these writings, it has not stopped me from searching for my own mode of fiction.

Soul Mountain uses pronouns instead of characters, psychological perceptions instead of plot, and changing emotions to modulate the style. The telling of stories is unintended, and they are told at random. It is a novel similar to a travel diary, and also resembles a soliloquy. Should critics not acknowledge it as fiction, it is fiction by virtue of their negating it.

I have my doubts about the various theories on fiction, probably because I have yet to find a good writer who has benefited from the guidance of theorists. They either stipulate rigid models or create fashions. The form of a work of fiction, like fiction itself, is the creation of the author.

To begin with, the form of fiction was quite free. What are generally called plot and characterisation are just popularly agreed-upon concepts. If art fails to transcend concepts it is difficult for it to achieve vitality; this is why novelists are generally unwilling to explain their work.

I am not a theorist. I am simply concerned with how to write fiction and with finding suitable techniques and forms.

Novelists' discussions of their craft and how they wrote a particular work often provide me with insights, and my talking about my own fiction is limited to this.

Both before and after the French *nouveau roman*, some writers created, or continued to search for, new fictional forms, and this search has not come to an end. The forms of modern Chinese fiction were imported from Europe at the beginning of the present century. Prior to the 1980s the narration of a fabricated story was stressed, but then there emerged a number of experimental writings which, influenced by Western modern fiction, were biased towards *how* a fabricated story was narrated.

In the fiction I wrote before *Soul Mountain* I was pursuing different narrative angles and methods. The seventeen short stories written between 1980 and 1986 and collected in *Buying a Fishing Rod for My Grandfather* are each different, and apart from the epilogue, all the stories had been published in literary journals in China. However, an editor afterwards explained that a directive from the authorities had banned the book's publication without any comment, so no publisher would touch it. It was not until 1988, through an introduction by a friend of mine, the Taiwanese writer Ma Sen, that it was published by Lianhe Publishing House in Taiwan. Ma Sen also helped with the publication of *Soul Mountain* in Taiwan, even though in the interim two publishers had rejected it, probably thinking it lacked market prospects.

When I started writing this novel I knew that it was predestined not to be a bestseller. The reason it took me seven years to complete was that I wanted it to achieve a great deal. In order to write it, I made three trips to the Yangtze River during 1983 and 1984, the longest of which was a journey of fifteen thousand kilometres. I had succeeded in working out the primary structure of the book, involving the first-person pronoun "I" and the second-person pronoun "you", in which the former is travelling in the real world while the latter, born of the former, is making a magical journey of the imagination. Later, "she" is born of "you", and later still the disintegration of "she" leads to the emergence of "he", who is the transformation of "I". This is the overall structure of the novel. It allowed me to observe the psychological levels of human language, which are in fact well suited to this type of structure, because human awareness of language begins with the emergence of pronouns. Chapters 51 and 52 discuss the structure and meaning of language in the novel.

The ancient Chinese concept of fiction was very broad: records of scenery and geography, records of people and the supernatural, *chuanqi* romances and historical tales, episodic novels, *biji* jottings and miscellaneous records were all considered fiction. In destroying the patterns of modern fiction I instinctively returned to tradition, and included all these genres in this novel of mine. While modern fiction strives mainly for a simple narrative method, I try to use a variety of methods, which I unify by changing pronouns. This corresponds with my understanding of language as constituting a flow. As a certain narrative method is mastered it is discarded, and as long as this does not damage the language, the flow is not interrupted. Such changes should be gradual and limited, otherwise the result could be complete chaos. It is music that helps me listen intently to the rhythm of my inner mind.

Of the eighty-one chapters of the book, it was only for Chapter 72 that I could not find the appropriate music. It was excruciating to write. In fact, this chapter is the key to the whole book. However, to place it at the beginning would have discouraged readers from even leafing through the book, and to remove it from the book would have meant I risked having an incomplete manuscript of only eighty chapters, like Cao Xuequin's *Story of the Stone*. I therefore simply added a sentence at the end: "Reading this chapter is optional ..."

To my mind, the popular isms of present times have little to do with the creative work of a writer. Generally, it is a case of a theorist's constructing his own theory and giving it a name. I refuse to attach an easily recognisable label to myself so that I will be included within a certain trend, and I certainly have no desire to establish a faction, form a group, or engage in partisan warfare. To say nothing of the anxiety, to do so often means putting aside one's serious creative writing.

The controversies in Chinese literature over the past century have virtually all been employed as gimmicks in political struggles, and ideological wars of words have replaced discussions of issues in literature itself. The struggles between isms have often resulted in new isms but no new writings. This pernicious cycle has, I fear, been a disaster for China's modern literature. If literary critics do not climb out of this demon bog it will be hard for any original ideas to emerge.

If Chinese exile literature writes only of exile, it does not have great prospects. Solzhenitzyn's precise dilemma was that he had pointlessly sacrificed his own fictional art by making war on a corrupt political regime, and in the process totally exhausted himself. Of all writers living in exile, I most appreciate Gombrowicz. He stood apart from all the trends and had no interest in isms; he had a profound hatred for fashions. He did not manufacture news or try to be sensational, but simply devoted himself to his vocation.

Some friends have said that *Soul Mountain* reveals a different Chinese culture. This was precisely what I set out to achieve. I believe that Chinese culture, broadly speaking, exists in four forms. The first is what is known as orthodox culture, and is associated with the Chinese Empire's generations of feudal monarchs, the Great Wall and the Imperial Palace, and the rare antiques connected with the lifestyles of emperors, kings, generals, ministers and scholars. For me, these are not the art of the common people. As in the case of Louis XIV era chairs, or Napoleon's hats, I propose that they be carefully preserved in museums — though it is not necessary to carry out restoration work on the Great Wall. Nor do I advocate the total abolition of the Confucian ethics and morality associated with that culture, and people who want to carry out research on these should be allowed to. Of course, there is also the associated Confucian literature, but evaluations were made long ago of the status and achievements of works such as *The Book of Songs*, *The Odes of Chu*, Han Dynasty *fu*, most of Tang poetry, the Song lyrics and the writings of the Eight Great Masters, as well as the eight-legged essays of the Ming and Qing dynasties.

The second form of culture is represented by Daoism, which has its origins in primitive shamanism, and Buddhism, which was reformed after its introduction from India. While at times promoted and patronised by emperors and kings, both retained independent forms that were religious but, unlike Western Protestant culture, never replaced political authority or encroached on orthodox culture. They therefore did not act as repressive agents in the development of Chinese culture; instead they often provided refuge for writers.

The third form is represented by folk culture: myths and legends, customs and practices, folk songs and folk music, the itinerant arts of singing, storytelling and dance, and the plays that developed from sacrifices, as well as the *huaben* stories.

The fourth form represents a purely Eastern spirit. This is largely manifested in the nature-based philosophies of Laozi and Zhuangzi, and the metaphysics of the Wei and Jin dynasties. It is also embodied by Chan Buddhism, which came many centuries later and, once divested of religious trappings, was a mode of life scholars could adopt in order to flee political oppression.

As for modes of material production in Chinese cultural life generally, these are comparable with those of other peoples in the world, so I will not concern myself with talking about them.

The culture in *Soul Mountain* is of course that of the latter three forms. While the first was at times spectacular, it stifled individuality, so that virtually all of the most richly creative writers and writings in China's classical literature originate from the latter three. *Soul Mountain* is imbued with a reclusive spirit, and it is in this respect that Eastern literature is different from that of the West. I think that if one wants to find connections between *Soul Mountain* and classical Chinese literary traditions, they lie primarily in its spirit. My preference was to go on a spiritual journey to reveal aspects of Chinese culture that had been concealed by bureaucratic orthodox culture.

I also believe that the Chinese civilisation derives from two major sources. The first is the Central Plains culture of the Yellow River Basin, whose existence has been widely acknowledged by historians for many generations. Confucian ethical rationalism, or what may be termed educating, is the essence of this culture.

At the same time a Yangtze River culture developed, almost in tandem. In recent years, historical research on Chu culture has expanded to encompass the Ba and Shu cultures of the Yangtze's upper reaches, and the Wu and Yue cultures of the lower reaches. Major archaeological findings have provided a wealth of materials, which have propelled some historians to a new understanding of the sources of Chinese culture and prompted them to initiate special research into the ancient cultures of the Yangtze River Basin.

One young academic has maintained that alongside these two cultures there existed the Haidai culture, which originated in the region along the coast of the Gulf of Bohai and Shandong Peninsula. The Hongshan culture, unearthed a few years ago in Liaoning Province, was another important discovery, but these regional cultures do not seem to have had a lasting impact on the history of Chinese culture. So I still regard the Yangtze River and the Yellow River as the two main sources of Chinese civilisation.

Over the past decades the unearthing of human fossils from the Paleolithic Age in the upper reaches of the Yangtze at Yuanmou has shifted the origin of the human species in China from the north to the south, and to more than a million years earlier. The uncovering of small stone artefacts from the Mesolithic Age in the Yuanmou region in the upper Yangtze and in the Jiangsu area in the lower Yangtze, as well as the discovery of the Hemudu culture, dating back seven thousand years to the Neolithic Age, testify to the fact that an ancient Yangtze River culture existed before that of the Yellow River Basin. The excavation at Hemudu of ivory carvings, wooden oars, palisade-style dwellings constructed on piles with wooden tenons, pottery dogs and human heads all indicate a more advanced culture than that of the Yellow River Basin.

Later on in history, the Majiabang and Liangzhu cultures of the lower Yangtze and the Daxi culture of the middle Yangtze developed simultaneously with the Yangshao and Longshan cultures of the Yellow River. The Daxi culture's stone carvings of human faces are the earliest known bas-relief carvings in China, and uniform symmetrical triangles and fan shapes carved on the outer surfaces of hollow ceramic balls indicate that the Daxi people possessed rudimentary knowledge of geometrical and mathematical concepts. Even more intriguing is the fact that the circular bases of the black pottery vessels of the Liangzhu culture of the lower Yangtze, like the red pottery of the Daxi culture, have been found to include geometrical carvings of circles, triangles and squares, combined in specific ways. I believe that these different designs have meanings and can be regarded as the earliest abstract signs in ancient China; at the same time, they indicate that the middle and lower reaches of the Yangtze had already linked to form one large regional culture.

Colourful pottery spindles, similar to those of the Qujialing culture discovered at Jingshan in Hubei Province, were found in Sichuan Province; they feature designs like the Yin and Yang fish on the Eight Trigram Chart. Moreover, the bronzes discovered in the middle and lower reaches of the Yangtze are not inferior to those of the Yellow River, and the Sanxingdui site artefacts unearthed at Guanghan, in Sichuan Province, are infinitely superior to all the bronze sacrificial vessels hitherto discovered on the Central Plains of the Yellow River. How was the brilliant culture of the Yangtze Basin destroyed? There is no record of this in historical texts!

It had always been thought that the legendary Xia culture was located on the Central Plains, but I once visited an excavation site at Erlitou in Henan Province where archaeologists showed me a large number of finely made, uniform earthenware items that were probably ritual vessels. Did they belong to the Xia culture, or to another culture of the same period? Either way, I believe I saw traces there of remote antiquity's patriarchal thinking.

I have no affinity for those northern cultures of the Yellow River Basin, but prefer to wander in the Yangtze Basin to search for that other culture, which I believe gave birth to the myths and legends of *The Classic of Mountains and Seas*. In recent times, this ancient shamanistic book, which fuses myth, legend, geography and history, was studied in detail, first by Meng Wentong and then by Yuan Ke. They both provided textual evidence that it originated either in the states of Ba and Shu or in the state of Chu. There is also a theory that the book passed through the hands of the Yue people, but that would still mean it originated in the Yangtze Basin. Not long ago certain scholars decided that the phrase "the highest peak of the Zhong Mountains" referred to Mount Tai in northern China, and irresponsibly added this annotation without any understanding of the book. At the time there was an urgent need for political unity, and the theory instantly became fashionable.

It would seem that during China's mythical period in the latter part of the Neolithic Age, prior to the Xia dynasty, the many tribes of the Yangtze Basin were already flourishing, and that most of the myths of remote antiquity, whose written records only date from Han and pre-Han times, originated from these tribes. Afterwards, the Yellow Emperor's tribes on the middle and upper reaches of the Yellow River grew more powerful. They fought endlessly with the tribes of the Yan Emperor before seizing a position of hegemony. As for the legend in which Yu the Great curbs the flood, this was yet another successful war of the Qiang tribes of the northwest against the various tribes of Miao barbarians and the Hundred Yue in the south.

It was only afterwards that cultural history was replaced by the bloodlines of emperors and kings, and later still, generations of Confucian scholars transformed culture into doctrine, so that China's ancient cultures became totally obscured. Now the pens of modern revolutionary historians have turned history into expositions of class warfare theory and patriotism, and research into the debacle of the feudal imperial system, foreign invasions and peasant uprisings has replaced research into cultural history.

I think a history of the Han culture needs to be written, dealing with its origins and the changes that have since taken place. To do so is beyond my capabilities, so I can only wait for specialist academics. All the futile controversies over the past century about China's cultural traditions would best be replaced by serious research on what is called tradition. The most creative writers, artists, thinkers, scientists and inventors have seldom been Confucians, and most of them have gained sustenance from the culture of the Yangtze River. This culture has retained its vitality because historically it has never occupied a position of orthodoxy, and also because of this vast region's unique cultural and geographical environment and the long history of the land itself. Of course, I am not saying that the Yellow River Basin and other regions of China have not possessed wonderful cultures. I am simply pointing out that the flourishing of culture has never been inextricably linked with political authority, and that culture has its own history.

The importation of modern Western culture does not mean that contemporary Chinese literary creation will cut ties with its own cultural traditions. I am not anti-culture, but I reject the "searching for roots" label, because my roots have been under my feet from the time of my birth. It is simply a matter of how I understand these roots, including how I understand myself.

I have studied inscriptions from the ancient states of Ba and Shu, the bird script on Yue swords and the silk paintings of Chu tombs. I have investigated the ancestral sacrifices carried out by Miao shamans, and I have listened to the Yi classics sung by their *bimo* priests. I have wandered along the Yangtze, from the giant panda reserve that is the home of the Qiang people right down to where it meets the China Sea, and from folk customs and practices I have returned to urban life. I was searching for self-realisation and a mode of living for myself.

For me, history remains an engulfing fog, and this self of mine makes me equally anxious. I look at Han culture in this way because I am a product of this culture.

I thank Professor Malmqvist for translating *Soul Mountain* into Swedish, and I thank Professor Lodén for organising this lecture.

The Modern Chinese Language and Literary Creation

Lecture delivered at the Modern Chinese Literature conference organised by the Aix-en-Provence Municipal Library, 3 November 1996

IT WILL BE HARD FOR WESTERN writers to comprehend the magnitude of the changes in the Chinese language — the language used in literary creation — that have taken place over the course of this last century. The transition from the classical language to the vernacular language virtually amounted to a linguistic revolution.

Modern vernacular writings have come from three sources: (1) the classical language, which had already undergone a process of becoming half-classical and half-vernacular during the late Qing and early Republican periods; (2) Ming and Qing storytellers' fiction and folk ballads, which were based on the spoken language — that is, from popular literature; and (3) the creations of Western-influenced writers since the May Fourth period. To a large extent, the language used in modern Chinese literature has resulted from the efforts of several generations of writers since the new literature movement of the May Fourth period.

The classical Chinese language does not have strict grammatical rules as Western languages do; it has only discussions and glosses of words used in texts. The first book of Chinese grammar, *Mr Ma's Comprehensive Grammar*, was written by Ma Jianzhong at the end of the nineteenth century, and despite the four-thousand-year history of the Chinese written language, the grammatical concepts of Western languages were foisted upon it in an attempt to explain it. Chinese language teaching in China continued as before, because teachers could not understand this newly compiled grammar. However, even after the vernacular came into use as the basis for the written language, research into the grammar of modern Chinese continued to follow Ma Jianzhong's old guidelines — although new concepts of modern Western linguistics were introduced in revisions and rewritings. This research ignored the actual teaching and writing of the language in China and has been an area strictly confined to linguists.

During the past decade a new generation of linguists, such as Shen Xiaolong, began questioning this approach and directing their energies towards ascertaining the linguistic structure of Chinese from within the language itself. This has brought about a revival in linguistics, but for writers, whose field is literary creation, it has been of little consequence.

The morphology and syntax of Western languages have been brought into the modern Chinese language through Chinese translations of Western works, especially through a vast quantity of poorly executed "hard" translations. In the course of accepting Western cultural influences, modern Chinese literature introduced the grammar of Western languages into literary writing, and thus over time caused written Chinese to become Europeanised. There were May Fourth writers who advocated "hard" translations — for instance, Lu Xun — but their solid grounding in the classical language and classical literature allowed them to neutralise foreign sentence patterns in their literary creations. And even when at times they happened to write a few Europeanised sentences it was not offensive.

From the 1950s on, the Chinese characters themselves were progressively simplified, which resulted in a gradual impoverishment of both commonly used characters and the spoken vocabulary. Then the Cultural Revolution occurred. During the liberalisation of the 1980s, just as China's contemporary literature was beginning to recover, it was again assailed by translations and critiques of contemporary Western literature. Even modern Western linguistic research and the theories of literary criticism based on it directly influenced Chinese literary creation. Few of the new generation of writers have had substantial training in classical Chinese, and the extent of Europeanising in their writing is quite serious. If one opens any literary magazine one will find it full of corrupt and nonsensical Chinese, especially in the case of modern poetry and avant-garde fiction. After constant exposure, people stop thinking it is odd, and end up believing Chinese can be written however it suits the writer.

Part of the problem stems from the fact that single characters form the basic units of the Chinese language, and the structure itself is thus highly versatile. Characters and sentences can be randomly organised, as long as there are no incorrect characters, so that in this era of the death of the author, when any number of interpretations is possible, should such a Chinese work be studied as a text it is capable of generating endless wide-ranging empty talk. And thanks to the work of some critics who are trying to be trendy, such convoluted and unreadable writings actually do become subjects of discussion.

There is no doubt that the Chinese language must develop; like any other language, it is continually evolving. I do not object to using some Western narrative modes to enrich the modern language. However, foisting "hard" translations from Western languages onto Chinese is not the direction of my endeavours in the written language. On the contrary, I seek to broaden the expressive potential of the Chinese language, while striving for a pure form of modern Chinese. But what in fact constitutes pure modern Chinese is a big question. It not only involves vernacular writing since the May Fourth period, but also goes back to the source of the ancient Chinese language.

Does the Chinese language, past or present, have a stable grammatical structure? In Chinese, words are made up of single characters, and the gender, number and case inflections found in Western languages do not exist. Nouns, verbs, adverbs and adjectives can automatically function as different parts of speech. Verbs do not conjugate: there are no distinctions of time, voice or mood, so there are no morphological changes to indicate the past, present or future, direct or indirect speech, condition or supposition. Subject and predicate are not always determined by word order, so there can be considerable freedom. The subject is often dispensed with, and it can be difficult to distinguish between a sentence without a subject and a sentence without a pronoun. Active and passive voice, and present and past participles do not exist. Relative clauses do not require conjunctions, and compound sentences have no time or voice restrictions. The relationship between words or between sentences does not require grammatical collocation, and is often concealed by implication and by the tone of words or sentences.

Thus in the Chinese language there is no trace of the most important syntactical forms of Western languages. This characteristic naturally provides the Chinese language with a high degree of versatility, and of course it does not require a great deal of effort to apply Western grammar to the Chinese language in order to write a very Europeanised version of Chinese.

Trying to work out the linguistic structure of Chinese from the functions of the Chinese language itself is fascinating, as well as difficult. But it could bring about a breakthrough in the discipline of linguistics, which was established mainly via the analysis of Western language types. I am well aware that this task is beyond me, but there are in fact people in the Chinese linguistic world currently engaged in this work. I have no wish to impose rules on myself for writing modern Chinese, and I constantly strive to make breakthroughs in what I write. All I can do is note how the linguistic structures of Chinese and Western languages differ, and look for modern forms of expression that are in harmony with the unique features of the Chinese language.

I set for myself one basic principle: it is I who speak the language, not the language speaking me. My searching in language is to allow me to articulate my perceptions and thoughts with greater accuracy and to prevent the language from manipulating me. Nowadays, with computers, it is becoming easier and easier to play word games; not just words and phrases, but even whole sentences can be shuffled like mah jong tiles then rearranged in different combinations. Because the single-character words of Chinese do not change according to syntax, such language games, even conceptual games, can be played with greater ease than in Western languages, although no human perceptions are involved in these words and sentences. This form of "linguistic Dadaism" has arrived in China a century after it arrived in the West. A hundred years ago the overturning of semantics by Dadaism was meaningful as social rebellion, but this is no longer the case in the postmodern West of today.

I do not indulge in games of semantic analysis. Deconstructionist literary theory that has been built on grammatical analysis is certainly clever, and can be useful for interpreting texts and for linguistic research. However, if this sort of textual study is used as a compass for creative writing, whatever is written will lack vitality. The writer Marlowe said a long time ago that art relies on the emotions, not the intellect.

What I seek is a language that is full of life, and in language what I seek is human feelings. Therefore the tone and feel of the language are more important to me than the choice of words and the construction of sentences. If it is the case that the ancient Chinese language is meticulous in rhetoric and esteems literary excellence, whereas in modern Chinese the clever manipulation of sentences is the fashion, then I would prefer to search for vibrant sounds in ordinary speech. Indeed, I regard this as the soul of what I write.

I have set out to rediscover language. I refer here to the language we are familiar with in everyday life, what is spoken and heard, not the lifeless sayings of ancient books. A huge number of such sayings have accumulated in the Chinese language and can be readily chosen for use in any situation. The modern Chinese language also contains an excessive number of neologisms and a new batch emerges every few years; for instance, an explanation of the term "cultural revolution" and the vocabulary of the decade of the Cultural Revolution would fill a handbook. This is because it is too easy to create words from Chinese characters. In my writing I avoid neologisms and popular sayings, except when they provide a fresh perspective within a particular linguistic context.

In my case, rediscovering language involves listening intently to what I write. If I fail to hear music in the sentences I have written, I acknowledge defeat, and discard or rewrite them. I talk in front of a tape recorder for my first draft, and when revising the manuscript I silently intone what I have written. All living languages have a musical quality, and testing this quality through listening to one's words is a good way of filtering out impurities. If language is offensive to the ear or is incomprehensible when read aloud, either it has been clumsily written or else the content is nonsense. If the writer is muddle-headed, will he be able to convey anything?

Sound is inherent to language, whereas writing came later. The written language is a form of recording. Calligraphy that evolved from Chinese characters is a form of visual art, not linguistic art. If the language of a written work lacks vitality, then however often lines of poetry are pulled apart and put together, or however often the words of a work of fiction are printed in different fonts, or the layout and printing attempt to be artistic, it cannot salvage the language. My writings strive to stand the test of being read aloud. This applies not just to my plays but also to my poetry and fiction.

For me, writing is foremost a search for the music of language, and then a search for content, characters, structure and reflection. However, the less naked reflection the better; it should be dissolved into the music of the lines of writing. Writing begins with a search for the music of language and everything else must be thought out before the writing begins. Whenever I start writing a new work I must search anew for language with the right appeal.

The musicality of language is of extreme importance, and music provides me with more insights than any sort of literary theory. When I write I always first select music that I want to hear, for it is music that helps me enter the state of mind and mood required for writing. Once the language with the right charm and rhythm has been found, the sentences to be recorded or written become audible, like musical phrases, and are no longer an arrangement of concepts and views dependent on thinking.

I believe that the inherent nature of language does not lie in description. Language, unlike painting, is not a visual art. It is impossible to depict the form and colour of a leaf, and when such a description is formulated in language, the more detailed it is the more difficult it is to recognise the leaf. Language is incapable of reproducing visual images; it is only through prompting or suggestion that it evokes associations in people's experiences. This is because the basic units of language are words, and a word is already an abstraction of a concept. The word "cup" is a composite concept of countless cups. Specifying that it is a big cup, a glass or a black pottery cup is enough. When talking about what one has observed about a cup, it is much more effective to explain it than to try to describe it. Strictly speaking, it is impossible to accurately describe scenery or a person's face, and what is evoked can only be impressions, not visual images.

Naturally, language can be articulated in countless ways, but literature requires a language for evoking feelings, not for discussion. Literary language and the discourse required of science differ because the latter seeks to eliminate subjective perceptions in order to define parameters, draw inferences and make judgments. Writing an academic paper in Chinese is like using a rational Western language, and perhaps requires some degree of Europeanisation, because the Chinese language is too fluid and can easily lead to ambiguity. It is certainly possible to use the Chinese language to define parameters and explain concepts, but it requires much greater attention to linguistic considerations.

Psychological analysis in contemporary Western literature must conform to the strict distinctions in tense, voice and mood of European languages. Contrastingly, to stress all these layers in Chinese — past, present and future tense, direct and indirect speech, condition, supposition, possibility and reality — would make the writing very clumsy. The ancient Chinese language does not distinguish between tenses, and what emerges in classical poetry and lyric could be called a psychological state that transcends time and space.

In China's traditional storytelling fiction, psychological activities were revealed through the actions of the characters. However, it would seem that the current Chinese language is inadequate for probing psychological activities and the subconscious, and for articulating them in language. Can a more fluid form of communication be found while respecting the inherent structure of the Chinese language, instead of bloating it with the tenses of Western languages? I have discovered a method of writing that I have called a "flow of language".

Stream of consciousness was developed in modern Western literature to capture the flood of psychological activities of an instant. Joyce and Woolf both wrote differently, and while unfortunately I can only read their work in translation and it is hard for me to fully savour it, I expect that their English language is exquisite. Proust and Brecht also used different methods of writing to articulate their psychological perceptions, but both were strict in their use of the French language and I have no problems experiencing the taste and musicality of the language itself. But how can one find a type of modern Chinese that will map the process of psychological activities without losing the musicality of the language?

Any language involving sound has to be actualised in a flow of linear time, as is the case with music. This is the ultimate limitation of linguistic expression, because people's conscious and subconscious are multidirectional. Like music, drama can be polyphonic, but it is impossible for other literary writings to transcend this linear flow. If language describes, explains and analyses, the stream of perceptions is interrupted. Art in language must acknowledge what it can do and what it cannot do if it is to reach its full potential. So, in tracking psychological activities, I prefer to dispense with the static language of discussion and relate only perceptions.

Yet language possesses a unique property, despite being linear. In particular language contexts, if the writer can create them, the meanings beyond the words create a tension that induces a feeling, an atmosphere or a psychological space, another dimension as found in music and drama.

The Chinese language does not indicate tense and often dispenses with the subject, and the order of the subject and predicate is relatively flexible. Attributives and complements, principal clauses and subordinate clauses seldom make use of binding conjunctions and prepositions. These features of the language closely approximate the way feelings are formulated, and make Chinese convenient for presenting psychological activities, which are inherently non-rational.

It is not that it is impossible for language to provide visual images. But the function of language is more to suggest than to describe. My short story "In an Instant" is a work in which I sought to use language to evoke visual images, including images of the mind. It borrows the use of a pair of neutral eyes and avoids words and sentences that bear any emotional colouring or subjective judgment, and the language is extremely concise and easy to follow. The heightened succinctness and clarity of words and sentences allow increased space for the reader's imagination, so that the visual images evoked are more vivid.

I strive for transparency in the Chinese language. I eliminate adjectives and other attributives where possible and separate into short sentences any components that clutter up the principal clause. In compound sentences I try to do away with conjunctions so that the relationship between clauses is hidden. I discard all non-essential elements in sentences, such as adverbial and verbal suffixes, and make every Chinese character carry out a vital function. When a monosyllabic verb can replace a disyllabic verb with the same meaning I will use the monosyllabic verb. Originally the Chinese language used mainly monosyllabic words; the existence of some tens of thousands of monosyllabic Chinese characters bears testimony to this. Seeking to minimise the use of compound words has helped me rediscover the inherent appeal of Chinese characters, each of which is an individual word.

Chinese culture does not emphasise logic and reasoning. Instead, it prizes spirituality and instinct, and this is largely related to the absence of grammatical forms and the versatile structure of the Chinese language. Thinking in the Chinese language easily leads one to bypass parameters, analysis, deduction and inference, and instead proceed directly to judgments and conclusions. Eastern culture developed from Daoist nature-based philosophy, Confucian ethics, Buddhist mind-nature and the Chan sect's use of language to reject language, whereas that of the West developed from logic and reasoning, coupled with Western Protestantism's precision and scientific approach. Therein lies the reason for the vastly different orientations of the two cultures.

It is not my intention in this short essay to discuss the relationship between the linguistic structures of these two great cultures. I am simply stating that when thinking and expressing oneself in Chinese one tends to overlook the process of deduction, and instead goes directly to a particular state or place. The mental images and sentiments found in China's classical poetry and prose are able to transcend Western time and space because they are spiritual states. Herein lie both the strength and weakness of the classical Chinese language. In my experience, thought and expression in the classical Chinese language are undoubtedly compact, and the language is exquisite, but it can easily cause thinking to short-circuit.

Writing, reading and the actualisation of language are all psychological activities. To observe and make comments about an object are not passive acts; a person is not like a camera, which does nothing more than mechanically release a shutter on a lens. The eyes of the person behind the camera are constantly choosing images and adjusting the focus, and both the line of vision and the focus are always shifting. If one uses language to describe an image in front of one's eyes, it is a process, even a so-called objective description. But in the eyes of a living person there are no purely objective images; even if the person is detached there are inevitably feelings, and an image will evoke a certain response. To capture an image in language can be a very complex process, and because it relies on language the writing must include naming and making judgments and associations. Seventy-seven whole chapters of *Soul Mountain* are devoted to such observations; I was intent on finding a form of Chinese language that could express the psychological processes involved.

If language is used to capture the images of the mind it will be even more intricate, because those images are more ephemeral than what is seen in the external environment. Even as one pursues these images in language they will already have been transformed; these perpetual transformations are impossible to control, so pursuing them in language is virtually impossible. A number of contemporary writers have tried very hard to record dream states, but at most have managed only to summarise the dream or produce a few odd, disconnected words. I have totally abandoned the idea and do not attempt to describe dream states. I use only the impressions left by dreams and organise them into a flow of language. My intention is to arrange the images of dreams so that they keep appearing, keep changing, and like music are endowed with a rhythm. Chapter 23 of *Soul Mountain* writes of the impressions left by a dream.

I do not directly describe mental images, hallucinations, memory or imagination. What concerns me is tracking psychological feelings. Images are simply the words or phrases of sentences, but by inserting the images evoked by these words and phrases into a flowing succession of sentences that are unrestricted and do not contain too many unnecessary components, psychological feelings are conveyed in a series of short sentences and clauses without conjunctions: a process of sustained actualisation of language.

The Chinese language does not precisely distinguish tense. In fact the past, present and future, memory and imagination, feelings and reflections, reality, possibility and fantasy have no morphological indicators, but instead constitute direct speech of this instant. This seems to closely approximate psychological processes, which by their very nature transcend concepts of real time and space; it also has a unique linguistic appeal that I find intriguing.

In discussions with my French translator Noël Dutrait, I suggested that everything be rendered into direct speech and present tense. His response was that this would constitute very bad French. Clearly, Chinese and French are completely different. Being fully aware of the disastrous impact of Europeanised Chinese on the modern Chinese language, I abandoned this stupid idea of mine. The conclusion I drew was that for reform or creation in any language, the structure of the language must be respected. High praise for the French translation of *Soul Mountain* has been published in the major French newspapers and I do not need to repeat it here.

Following the vernacular literature movement, the Chinese language, formerly comprising single-character words, came to include more and more disyllabic or polysyllabic words. This augmented the existing four tones and the tonal patterns, allowing for enhanced musicality in the language. In my writing I especially seek after linguistic musicality. It was specifically for this reason that I rendered Li Qingzhao's lyrical poem "Every Sound Slow" into modern Chinese using very long sentences. Some key words motivated variations that lengthened the duration of feelings.

In my plays and fiction, I pay a great deal of attention to rhythm and tonal variations in the language, both in soliloquies and dialogues, and in narration. The way music is composed gave me a brilliant idea: if one could deal with language as if one were composing music, it would have greater potential to express emotions. I believe this is possible, especially since flexible word order and lack of tense restrictions allow the Chinese language to be written virtually like music. Some of the soliloquies and dialogues of my plays *Between Life and Death* and *Dialogue and Rebuttal*, for instance, were written as linguistic music, although not using traditional rhyme patterns. When narrative language resembles poetry it can also convey feelings; Virginia Woolf's *The Waves* and some of Marguerite Duras' work contain precedents. Georges Perec's long poem *I Remember* does the reverse, inserting narrative language into poetry. My recent play *Weekend Quartet* has directly borrowed from a musical form. To write it, I listened to no fewer than seventy or eighty quartets by composers ranging from Haydn and Mozart to Shostakovich, Messiaen and Gorecki. In writing one can gain huge insights from using musical forms, because the musicality of the modern Chinese language is no longer limited to rhyme, the four tones or the tonal patterns.

Large numbers of compound words have appeared in the modern Chinese language. New words and phrases formed from two or more characters have naturally resulted from the new things and concepts of modern life, because the existing vocabulary of the language was inadequate. However, the widespread use of polysyllabic words has caused people to neglect the four tones and the tonal patterns of Chinese, and this is why arbitrarily created words often sound odd. In my writing I emphasise the rediscovery of Chinese characters, especially the appreciation of monosyllabic verbs, because this helps reinforce the musicality of the language. Whether or not writing in modern Chinese can be easily read aloud depends precisely on the writer's reacquainting himself with the phonology of the language.

I do not indiscriminately use or arbitrarily create vocabulary and phrases, and I do not use archaic words. Many words died with the books of the remote past that contained them and are only used when quoted by scholars. I write in the living language. Commonly used words need to be appreciated again; when they are infused with the individual's pulsating feelings even these banal characters and words can still have strong expressive power.

I am also interested in adopting lively terms from the standard spoken language and from dialects, without regional limitations, ranging from those of Beijing, Sichuan and Jiangxi, as well as the Nanjing standard language, to the dialects of the Wu language. However, I use them on the condition that they will be understood when heard or read by someone who does not understand that dialect. I do not write literature in a specific dialect and I do not use dialects to create a specific local flavour. I use them only to enrich my vocabulary, in order to expand the expressive potential of the modern Chinese language. It must be borne in mind that the reason why the Chinese in use at present has such rich and lively expressive power is that over the past century generations of writers have infused the dialects of various regions into it.

The Chinese language is more versatile and much more concise than Western languages. But very long sentences can still be written, and there are many examples in ancient Chinese. Unfortunately, in contemporary Chinese writings there are huge sentences that often use structures not inherent in the Chinese language but modelled on poor translations of modern Western writings. In such translations, complex sentences that are structurally linked and hard to break up in the original work are translated as strings of lifeless sentences, or sentences that are not sentences, because equivalent expressions could not be found in Chinese. Moreover, punctuation is not added. The translators must undoubtedly bear responsibility for these cavalier works, which any Western language editor would find unacceptable. The problem is that some writers who were unable to read the originals have read these rough and irresponsible translations and wrongly assumed that the great modern writers of the West actually wrote like this. Imitating these bad translations suddenly became trendy, leading to the terrible corruption of the modern Chinese language.

This has been my experience. Since I use the Chinese language for my writing, to change it I would have to begin from within the structure of the Chinese language itself; I would have to find mechanisms that I could develop. I have learned much from the essays of Han Yu and Jin Shengtan, and from *Midnight Songs of the Wu Region*, compiled by Feng Menglong. China's traditional lyrical poetry and songs, the folksongs of the Wu dialect region south of the Yangtze and the storytelling and ballad singing of Suzhou are storehouses of colourful, dynamic Chinese. At present, Chinese avant-garde literature is absorbing modern Western literary concepts. If it draws nourishment from these Chinese-language sources at the same time, I am sure modern literary innovations will greatly enrich the Chinese language, without damaging its phonology or sensuousness.

To recapitulate, since literature is a way of describing man's existence and surroundings, it is invariably associated with vibrant human feelings. If the language of literature is not supported by the feelings of living people, and is only form for the sake of form or language for the sake of language, it is highly likely all that will remain of it in the future will be an empty shell of language that in time will turn into a heap of linguistic garbage.

Ancient Greek tragedy and Shakespeare, Cervantes' *Don Quixote*, Dante's *Divine Comedy*, Goethe's *Faust*, Kafka and Joyce employ different linguistic forms but all continue as testimonies of human existence. The writings of Li Bai and Cao Xueqin have not died out either, because their language too can still evoke true feelings in people of today. One can never say everything about truth; it can never be exhausted — and this is probably why literature continues to exist. People of both ancient and modern times have striven to use their own languages to articulate the existence of this truth. But truth can only be perceived by the individual; there is no general unified truth. The boundless richness and vibrancy of literature lie hidden in the perceptions of the individual. In modern times literature has been subjected to waves of bombardment by various isms and by theories proclaiming the death of literary predecessors, but these have failed to destroy it.

Literary creation is also a way of life. Through writing, an author gets closer to the truth of his own life and to an understanding of himself and the world. What every writer searches for, it should be said, is simply a unique language that he can use to express his own feelings. It is quite normal to find differences in literary language among the large numbers of writers who write in the same language; the only thing they have in common is that they are all bound by the grammatical rules of that language.

To talk extravagantly about some national literature is not very meaningful, except for the political needs of the nation, which have very little to do with literature. Literature transcends national boundaries, but it is difficult for it to break through the limitations of the language in which it is written, and whatever language is used will leave its imprint on a literary work. Apart from differences in social history and lifestyle, it would seem that the characteristic of the national culture most deeply imprinted on literature is the language in which the writer perceives and articulates. The differences between the cultures of the East and West, I think, are due to the different modes of thinking created by the different languages. This is because human cultural history also includes religious beliefs, which have to be actualised through a specific language framework.

The poetic nature of language does not derive solely from the expression of emotion. When one focuses one's gaze and listens, a tension is created, and it is in this that poetry is found. When one concentrates on something external to oneself or on an image in one's mind, then expresses this in language, the language will be pregnant with poetry, and if one listens to the language one is writing and silently intones it like a performer playing a musical instrument, or like a singer listening to his own voice, the language comes to life and is endowed with a poetic quality, or a soul.

By concentrating one's gaze and listening intently, what one writes will spring to life out of the pit of traditional rhetoric. The modern Chinese language must jump out of the prison of ancient prose and not atrophy in the old trap of playing with words. It is essential for the language to be rediscovered and endowed with a sense of being alive.

With its long prose-essay tradition, it is also possible for Chinese literature to introduce the language of prose essays into the writing of contemporary fiction. In my novel *Soul Mountain* I have tried to smash down the barriers between narration and the prose essay.

If the narrator listens to his own language he will discover that changing pronouns is not a game of clever writing. There is sufficient psychological basis for the three pronouns I, you and he to represent different narrative angles. I swap pronouns both in the narrative language of my fiction and in my plays. In fiction I do so to change the narrative angle, and in plays I do it to control the relationship between the actor and the role that he plays. However, this sort of switching cannot be arbitrary, especially in the Chinese language. In Western languages the changing of pronouns requires corresponding conjugation of verbs and morphological changes to the initiator of action and the receiver of the action, otherwise it will not be clear whether it is the person or the piano that is being played. But in Chinese the arbitrary switching of pronouns can lead to total chaos, just like the cacophony of an insane piano, and writings in modern Chinese frequently suffer from this sort of insanity.

I seek a pure form of modern Chinese, which of course is what every serious Chinese writer does. What I strive for is simply my own language; I have no plans to standardise Chinese.

The mode of language adopted does not define a creative work, but searching for it proceeds in tandem with writing; once a work is completed, the language will have been found.

In fact, during the process of writing there is much that is not written into a work. Language can only articulate a minute portion of a person's feelings; a huge part is lost. For this reason, I believe what I write is still far removed from what I actually feel, but I can only try to use language to get as close as possible to this truth.

This is what I wildly hope to achieve — but people live with all sorts of wild hopes, and perhaps even knowledge of the self is one of these. Yet if people did not have some small degree of wild hope, I think nothing would ever be achieved, and there would never be this thing that we refer to as literature.

About *Fleeing*

16 May 1991, Stockholm (speech presented at a play reading at the Swedish Royal Theatre)

FOLLOWING THE TIANANMEN events of 1989 a friend asked if I would write a play about China for an American theatre company; it would of course have to do with real life. I agreed. In August the first group of refugees who had fled Beijing arrived in Paris, and among them were several of my good friends. I started to write the play at the beginning of September and a month later I submitted my manuscript. After reading the English translation the theatre company requested changes, but I refused. I asked my friend to explain to them that when I was in China the Communist Party could not coerce me into making changes to my manuscripts, so an American theatre company certainly would not. The Swedish Royal Theatre is now enthusiastic about performing the play, and for this I would like to express my heartfelt thanks.

The play appeared in the first number of the Chinese periodical *Today*, after it resumed publication, but overseas. From information recently received from China, I learned that the authorities had listed the periodical as a reactionary publication, and that I had been expelled both from the Chinese Communist Party and from my state appointment. I must add that they were too late in making that decision, because I publicly announced my resignation from the Chinese Communist Party two years ago in Paris, when the first shots of the massacre were fired.

This play of mine was also criticised by some activist friends from the Democracy Movement. That was only to be expected, since the play attacked certain infantile aspects of the Movement. Some writer friends criticised the play from another angle: they thought it was too political and not a purely literary work. I definitely am not a political activist and do not consider that literature has any need to be subservient to politics, but this does not preclude me from discussing politics in my writings at times if I want to. It is simply that I do not approve of the sort of biased writing that ties literature to the war chariot of a particular faction, because as a writer one has one's own things to do.

My reasons for writing this play were not confined to condemning the massacre. I stated in my introductory note that it is not a socialist–realist play. As I see it, life is a state of perpetual fleeing, from political oppression or from others. One must also flee from one's self, because once the self has been awakened it is this that one cannot flee; this is the tragedy of modern man.

In his book *Ode to Fleeing*, the modern French thinker Henri Laborit says that if resistance forms a group, the individual resister is instantly reduced to subservience within the group, so his only solution is to flee. I agree with his way of thinking. In my view, the unwavering independence of the individual is of the utmost importance for a writer, or for any person, otherwise what freedom is there? For the writer, fleeing is not at all unusual. I have calmly accepted this reality, and in the remaining years of my life I do not aspire to return to a so-called homeland ruled by a tyrannical government.

As well as springing from political repression, social customs, the fashions of the times and the will of others, I think a person's misfortune originates from the self. This self is not God. It should not be repressed, nor should it be exalted; it is simply as it is. But fleeing from it is impossible; this is the fate of humankind. The Greek tragedies dealing with fate, the Shakespearean tragedies about the individual and modern tragedies concerned with the self of modern man are in fact all derived from the same source, and this was why I gave my play the form of a pure tragedy.

I suggested that naturalist or realist methods not be used in the performance of *Fleeing*. Instead, I recommended that it be performed as demonstrated in today's reading of my play *Soliloquy* by Mr Björn Granath, who will direct *Fleeing*. The actor should maintain a certain distance from the character he is playing, observing that character from that distance, and entering and departing from it from time to time. Theatricality and appropriate ritual in the performance are both essential. Over the past few days I have worked with the director, theatre personnel, choreographer and actors on rehearsal plans. It is a great relief that they understand what I want.

At a gathering of some Chinese writers in Oslo last year, I said that in this modern age, with its growing flood of film and television, literature — that is, non-consumerist literature — is increasingly becoming a matter for the individual. I also said that writing is a luxury, particularly for those writing in Chinese and living in exile, and they have to be able to endure the loneliness. I did not imagine that so many people would be present at this gathering today, and for this I thank all of you. I also thank Professor Göran Malmqvist, who has translated *Fleeing* into Swedish.

The Voice of the Individual

4 April 1993, Paris (paper presented at the Nation, Society and the Individual symposium held at Stockholm University)

I AM HIGHLY SUSPICIOUS WHENEVER the name of a collective is invoked; I actually become afraid that this collective name will strangle me before I have the chance to say anything. "Chinese intellectuals" is a collective noun that I cannot, of course, represent, and I am terrified that if it represents me I will be annihilated. However, it happens to be one of the issues for discussion today, and it may be said to be a very important issue.

In the period from the failure of the Hundred Day Reforms in 1898 to the 1911 Revolution, what were known in the West as intellectuals began to appear in China. Before that, in my view, China's intellectual class consisted only of scholars or gentry, who, while greatly concerned about individual conduct and about literature, also emphasised the spiritual. They esteemed moral perfection, but that morality was limited to Confucian ethical standards. The nature-orientated philosophy of the Daoists led to non-action, and the nirvana of the Buddhists further eroded individuality. Neither the eccentric behaviour of the famous scholars of the Wei and Jin dynasties nor the sprouting of urban culture at the end of the Ming dynasty were able to provide the Chinese intellectual class with the soil that could produce individualism. Individualism is in fact a recent product of the rationalist traditions of Western Protestant culture and the subsequent flourishing of capitalism.

Chinese intellectuals did not form a social class that was independent of the ruling power until the new culture movement of the May Fourth period, following the collapse of feudal imperialism and the flooding of Western thinking into China. An awareness of modern individualism came about with the introduction of Western political thinking; it primarily fulfilled a political need, and the need to acknowledge the value of an individual's spiritual activities was secondary. The result was that Chinese intellectuals, as individual thinking persons, came to speak to society in the name of the individual.

However, this ideal situation did not last. By the 1930s, just a decade later, domestic turmoil, foreign threat, revolution and war again hopelessly embroiled Chinese intellectuals in political struggles to save the nation and the people. Whether they were aware of it or not, and perhaps for reasons beyond their control, they transformed themselves into the tools of political factional fighting, or were used as tools by the political factions. Although small numbers of them tried to maintain their independence, it was difficult for them to continue thinking and writing. This has been the tragic experience of China's modern intellectual class from its very inception.

These circumstances meant that at the same time as affirming their spiritual worth as individuals, Chinese intellectuals had to free themselves from the tenacious grip of political conflict. Unlike their Western counterparts, it was hard for them to separate learning and literary creation from politics, and to be able to fully realise their personal worth in the realm of purely spiritual activities. Either they entered politics or they were subjected to political harassment, and for close to a century there has been interminable political turmoil. Today Chinese intellectuals are reviewing history not to blame their predecessors, but to find a way of extricating themselves from this nightmarish predicament. This, I think, is a good starting point for discussion of the problem.

Criticism of history cannot replace criticism of present reality, and criticism of present reality cannot replace present reality itself. The present reality is that China's intellectuals remain in the same predicament. There is still no guarantee of basic human rights such as freedom of speech, publishing and news reporting. When Chinese intellectuals who have gained such rights abroad research and discuss the general relationship between the individual, society and the state, they find it impossible to forget the specific situation in China, and they undertake their research on China's history and present reality in order to sort themselves out. Since they cannot change history and cannot save monolithic China, they would do well just to save themselves.

Is it a historical necessity for Chinese intellectuals to place the heavy burden of saving the nation and the race upon their shoulders at the same time as affirming their personal worth? Is it possible for Chinese intellectuals to have a slightly better fate? Is it possible *not* to be a saviour or a sacrifice while asserting the individual's value and independence? Under the totalitarian government of China these possibilities are indeed slight.

This is not to say that the elite of China's first generation of intellectuals did not champion the worth of the individual; indeed, the courageous effort and uncompromising stance of Lu Xun and Hu Shi remain unmatched by anyone in China's current intellectual world. However, not being able to take control of politics and instead falling foul of endless political faction fighting, Chinese intellectuals have suffered extreme hardship. Undeniably, political participation has been a matter of individual choice, but this widespread choice by Chinese intellectuals reveals an inherent weakness unrelated to China's social reality.

Having censured the deep-rooted nature of Chinese nationalism, it is now time to consider an inherent weakness in Chinese intellectuals themselves. The self-worth that was promoted with fanatical fervour during the May Fourth period made it generally difficult for Chinese intellectuals to withstand the onslaught of political tides, because this form of self-worth was a romantic sentiment, not a mature rational understanding of the notion. Its origins did not lie in the French rationalism of the Enlightenment but in Nietzsche's German philosophy of the Superman, so it was not true individualism but a tragic belief in the supremacy of the individual.

This newly awakened self was very fragile, and when suddenly confronted by the collective interests of the race, nation or class, it easily fused into a single entity — a bloated big self — that became the spokesperson of the race, nation or class. As a result, the spiritual autonomy of the individual was easily swallowed up by the collective will of the race, nation or class. Whether it was Lu Xun-style revolutionary radicalism, Hu Shi-style liberalism, Guo Moruo-style capitulation to communism or Zhou Zuoren-style surrender to imperialism, it all came under the flag of saving the nation and the people, even if at times the aim was only to save oneself. This self-interest is, I fear, characteristic of Chinese intellectuals, even if, from the standpoint of China's old intellectual class of scholars and upright gentlemen, the moral conduct of these individuals is beyond reproach.

Although Chinese intellectuals had to some extent been influenced by Western individualism, being the progeny of traditional Chinese literati culture they ultimately were not able to extricate themselves from the overweening influence of the ancestral land that was a part of traditional Chinese ethics. It must be recognised that it is this deeply entrenched patriotism that is the greatest psychological obstacle to any unwavering affirmation of the individual's worth by Chinese intellectuals.

Only the few who went abroad were able to overcome this obstacle and, by teaching in Western universities or finding some means to a livelihood away from their ancestral land, to maintain a certain degree of freedom in their writing and creative work. Yet whenever the feeling of patriotism assailed them they would rush back to their beloved homeland, where they would again fall foul of this predicament, or become utterly frustrated and despondent.

I see this sort of patriotism as a trap for Chinese intellectuals. What is nowadays called "China sentiment" is in fact a form of psychosis from which Chinese intellectuals must free themselves.

Chinese intellectuals have never clearly separated the concept of nation from their notion of the individual. Because individuality has always been repressed in China's traditional culture, any articulation of human rights will stop at the right to personal existence, and there are only ever very cautious attempts to encourage freedom in the spiritual activities of the individual. "The scholar may be killed but not humiliated" and "To kill oneself is benevolence" are sayings that refer to moral integrity, but are associated with the sacrosanct ethics of loyalty to the ruler, and have nothing to do with the individual's freedom of thought. As long as ideology is truth one can die without fear, and even if a Western ideology suddenly becomes the truth for saving the nation it will be similarly endowed with ethical lustre. Chiang Kai-shek's nationalism and Mao Zedong's communism were both empowered by reverting to the ethical traditions of feudal imperial China. It was therefore difficult for the fledgling individualism of Chinese intellectuals to ward off the onslaught of the totalitarian state, which had its foundations in this deep-rooted collective subconscious.

I believe that it is the responsibility of Chinese intellectuals today to destroy this modern myth of the nation. The reason why it is so difficult to affirm basic human rights, especially the right to freedom of thought, is because the burden of patriotism on Chinese intellectuals is too heavy. The nation's political authority has always restrained the individual by imposing the collective will, and beyond a certain point this is invasive and harmful to the individual's basic human rights, and amounts to repression. Whether it be in the name of the race or of the people, state dictatorships that infringe upon or deny the individual's right to freedom of thought are guilty of committing human rights crimes.

For almost a century the Chinese intellectual world has had no shortage of heroes who have been killed or freely sacrificed themselves for the nation, the people or even a political party, yet there have been very few to publicly proclaim their willingness to risk their lives for the sake of the individual's right to freedom of thought and self-expression. To rebel against one's ancestral land or become the enemy of the people is considered the most serious of crimes, and for Chinese intellectuals the psychological pressure of morality is harder to endure than being subjected to physical harm. This to some extent explains why many intellectuals of the left wing and within the Communist Party have willingly risked their lives for the nation and the revolution and why they rushed to acknowledge their crimes when the political authorities they had supported suddenly labelled them as rightists or counter-revolutionaries.

Chinese intellectuals opposed feudal ethics and political authority with extraordinary valour, yet when confronted by this modern superstition — the myth of the nation — they seemed to have their hands tied and be totally helpless. This was because the superstition had its source in the national psyche; it was more deeply rooted than any kind of ethics, and it was sustained by fear. In any confrontation it was the individual's life pitted against the huge national collective, and the individual's survival instinct made it impossible for him not to be terrified. The feudal empire had collapsed, but the feudal ethical system, with its web of loyalties to the ruler, had mutated into a race-based patriotic sentiment that exerted an equally powerful moral force. When those in control of the nation made use of the power at their disposal to activate all the machinery of propaganda, it was easy for them to manufacture such a fallacy. What the individual seemed to confront was no longer a finite number of people controlling them, but the whole nation, or rather that abstract notion that had been given the name of "the race" or "the people". This is a strategy commonly used in modern totalitarian politics. The more loudly catchwords like patriotism and nationalism are shouted the more suspect they are. Chiang Kai-shek's "The nation is supreme", and in more recent times Mao Zedong's "Dictatorship of the people", also came under the flag of patriotism.

If it is argued that for Chinese intellectuals the dream of an independent, wealthy and strong China has stifled freedom of thought, then their collective consciousness must be suffering from some congenital defect. This was first manifested as communist thinking began to take root in China: intellectuals failed to distinguish between those who work with the mind and other social classes, such as workers and peasants. They persisted in thinking of themselves as the spokespeople of the masses and thus often overlooked their own special rights. In fact, the spiritual work of the intellectual requires an affirmation of individual worth more than it requires the general economic, political and educational rights to which workers, peasants, labourers and merchants are also entitled.

On coming to power, the Chinese Communist Party had a far superior understanding of the need for this separation than the Chinese intellectuals, and it reduced the social status of intellectuals to below that of workers and peasants. However, from the 1930s Chinese intellectuals — not just the left-wing intellectuals, but also the many liberals who became Bolsheviks or who recast themselves as part of the masses —

began abrogating the right to freedom of thought that they had won during the May Fourth period. It may therefore be said that impoverishment of the thinking of Chinese intellectuals had set in prior to the dictatorship of the proletariat.

As a social class, Chinese intellectuals have not had a strong consciousness of themselves as individuals and generally have not confronted society as individuals, although a feeling of loneliness often revealed itself in Lu Xun's early writings. In fact, it is precisely in the uncompromising independence of the individual that the creative spirit lies. When the intellectual confronts society as an individual, his existence is more real. If the self of the intellectual is dissolved in the collective big self, or what is known as "we", the individual self no longer exists.

The position occupied by Chinese intellectuals at present requires that they first strive for their basic human rights as individuals living in modern times. Apart from the right to survival, these include the right to freedom of thought — that is, freedom to speak, write and publish without political sanctions and without having to pay a high price for this right.

After 1949 the Chinese Communist Party took charge of the livelihood of intellectuals, and, through its policy of reforming their thinking to the service of the people, took away their capacity for independent existence. Their right to independent thought was also restricted to increasingly narrow guidelines, as stipulated by the Party, with slight transgressions resulting in severe punishments. This therefore determined that any debates in the Chinese intellectual world became political struggles, even factional clashes within the Communist Party. In the fields of scholarship, literature and the arts, there could be no individual creations, because even these areas had been turned into tools of propaganda for the Party, and intellectuals themselves were carrying out orders as cogs in the national machinery under its leadership. This totalitarian politics reached a high point during the Cultural Revolution: intellectuals had no guarantee of space for a private life, their personal security could be threatened at any time, and countless numbers of them were branded as rightists.

Needless to say, intellectuals did not protest, and fleeing from this all-pervasive dictatorship was virtually impossible — apart from the exceptional case of the violinist and composer Ma Sicong. On the contrary, it was only from within the Party that the likes of the extraordinary veteran of the opposition faction, Chen Yi, with his intellectual origins, were bold enough to take a stand and retaliate. All of this took place in the name of the revolution, and later on the collective will was brought to an even higher level of concentration, which manifested itself as the worship of Mao Zedong's leadership. Lu Xun's being elevated to the status of a divinity was another outcome of this political need. Humankind's primitive superstitious belief in spirits re-emerged as a superstitious belief in the race, the nation and the leader. As an individual, the intellectual is neither a disciple nor a hero, and likewise, when threatened by the collective, Chinese intellectuals were unable to escape the physiological instinct of fear that is a universal human weakness.

In the 1980s Deng Xiaoping's policy of reform and opening up to the outside world meant the relaxing of stringent restrictions on thinking, literature and the arts, and as a result Chinese intellectuals gained a limited amount of private space. Alongside the political struggle for democracy, there was a resurgence in individuality and consciousness of the self, and Nietzsche's philosophy of the Superman, with its romantic notion of saving the world, once again became a powerful intellectual tide. And Chinese intellectuals once again re-enacted their historical roles, as heroes of the race and the nation, and as victims.

At the same time there began a new trend that represented a shift from the fight for the individual's space to exist to the fight for the individual's space for spiritual activities. This non-politicised wave of thinking amongst Chinese intellectuals, it should be noted, was also a political battle to get rid of the controls of government ideology, but it no longer linked the freedom of the individual with the fate of the nation and the race.

It was difficult at times to absolutely separate these two trends of thinking, and sometimes they would clash. When the latter was promoted the former often exerted moral pressure on it, and in the latter's ridiculing of the former it was often forgotten that what the latter promoted was only possible with the backing of the former. This clash of ideas within the ranks of Chinese intellectuals was due to the fact that they had not yet liberated themselves from the shadow of history.

I do not oppose intellectuals who go into politics. In my own case, while I have no intention of going into politics, I have no compunctions about publicising my political opinions. Political views, even political activities, can be associated with the individual intellectual's creative activities; the two areas are not mutually exclusive. Whether intellectuals go into politics, or simply devote themselves to pure scholarship or pure literature, is a matter of individual choice, and all sorts of choices are possible.

However, if all Chinese intellectuals are swept into politics then the misfortunes of the Chinese intellectual world since May Fourth will inevitably be repeated. I have heartfelt reverence for the many intellectuals who went to the extent of sacrificing their lives for the nation, the people and democracy, but I also grieve for those intellectuals who did not want to go into politics but through no crime of their own ended up committing their own scholarly and artistic lives to the grave. This generally has not constituted a problem for intellectuals in the West, but Chinese intellectuals have had to pay too high a price. My reflecting upon the history of Chinese intellectuals today is an attempt to somehow reduce the occurrence of such misfortunes.

I do not think that China will suddenly change before the end of the century and that Chinese intellectuals can expect work conditions in the near future that approach those of their counterparts in the West. In China, ideological controls on intellectuals have not been removed, and with the addition of the cultural commercialisation brought about by market economics, a twofold pressure has been created. If the present generation of Chinese intellectuals continue the old dream of their predecessors it will still be difficult for them to avoid becoming funerary objects in the political struggles of Party factions. The large numbers of Chinese intellectuals who went to live abroad in exile after the Tiananmen events of 1989 experienced an awakening, and if they were able to shake off that persistent China complex and do what they chose to do, it was an even greater awakening.

The spiritual creations of the intellectual are the acts of the individual. The individual will feel lonely within his social environment, but his creations will be more authentic than any created by some made-up collective, however wonderful its slogans.

Fleeing, of course, is by no means the purpose of life. It is merely a strategy for self-preservation. Under the weight of reality, even more important is spiritual fleeing. It is impossible for creative activities — culture — to transcend real existence, so what intrinsic value do they have? The difference between thought processes and animal instincts in humans is reflected in their capacity to imagine, and culture is the crystallisation of this. Human transcendence of matter and spiritual transcendence of the external world are totally dependent on this capacity, and it is only in the spiritual world created by the imagination that the freedom of the individual's consciousness can be fully realised.

However, given the circumstances of both past and present reality, when the individual seeks to realise his will, passionately imagining himself as a hero who will save the world but failing to think rationally about it, he will necessarily become a hero of the race and the people, and then a political martyr. If he demands that others be martyred along with him, this will amount to the collective suicide of China's intellectual world. In the fields of scholarship, literature and the arts, if the expression of the self expands to the exclusion of the choices of others, and the self only is revered as God, probably it can only lead to the individual's insanity.

Whether it is in the name of the collective, the race, the ancestral land or the people, the expansion of the individual's will and the unlimited bloating of the consciousness of the self manifest themselves as extremisms that will lead to the loss of freedom and the destruction of the self. While realising one's individual freedom, that of others must be respected, and this is in effect a limitation. The democracy of modern societies is founded on basic human rights that involve limited freedom. Responsibility and cooperation, respect and tolerance are necessary preconditions for realising the will of the individual and the expression of the self in modern societies.

Looking back at the numerous debates in the Chinese intellectual world over this past century, it would seem that it was hard to break out of the mould of negation for the sake of negation and criticism for the sake of criticism; this was also the case in re-evaluations of Chinese traditions. In the cultural thinking of China during the past hundred years, fighting has won over building up and criticism has won over creation. The violent principles of criticism and antinomy have considerably impoverished modern China's cultural thinking.

Tradition or reform, Chinese spirituality or Westernisation, to criticise or to inherit, Chineseness or modernity, literature or politics — for the sake of literature, life or the people; class nature, the nature of the people, the Party's nature, human nature or individuality — who is to arbitrate? Eastern or Western, authentic or inauthentic, form or content, realism or modernism, Third World or postmodernism, even modernism or postmodernism — all such debates are traps. The conditions, the arguments and even the conclusions of such debates are decided beforehand, and if one becomes involved one need not bother thinking about escaping. It is essential for Chinese intellectuals to break out of this mindset of fighting for quick solutions, to avoid the trap of debates and each go his own way, because these interminable disputes lead nowhere.

Throughout the past century the Chinese intellectual world has attempted to find the truth from the West. Let us for the time being not concern ourselves with whether or not truth exists. But the communism that swept the world from World War I until after World War II is bankrupt, and the socialism that was popular in Western Europe after World War II is in critical decline, while traditional Western liberalism, though surviving, is facing one crisis after another. Instead, it is racism that has suddenly reared its head. At a time when Chinese intellectuals are in the process of throwing off the myth of the nation and striving for political democracy, whether they will be able to avoid falling into the lair of racism again and to firmly uphold the independence of the individual's conscience remains problematic.

The present is a time when ideology has crumbled and theory has imploded. There are fashions every year, but they are changing more and more quickly, so that there is no longer a reliable mainstream. I think this might well be called a period of no isms, because ideologies have been replaced by ever-changing methodologies.

The only way for the individual to find a standpoint in this world is to doubt. What I refer to as "to doubt" is an attitude, not an ism. In constructing one's spiritual world, to doubt may be considered a standpoint to some extent. Since logic actualised through language is unreliable, linguistic narration provides nothing more than various possibilities. Moreover, the self only exists within a network of perceptions whose actualisation depends on their being expressed in language. In other words, the existence of the self is nothing but its expression in language, and the affirmation of the self is embodied in the existence of one's unique language. What one has expressed in language requires no verification, and indeed, verification is impossible. The individual comes to the world from the dark realm of the self via language and there is a certain amount of communication with others. If he does not somehow get himself killed, commit suicide or go insane, he will benefit from some form of rationality that is based on doubt.

I am a Chinese writer, only one person, and I cannot represent others. China for me is not that huge race or abstract nation; it is simply the cultural background that manifests itself in my writings, the culture's impact on me since my birth, and the modes of thought, nurtured by the Chinese language, that I use in my writings. I also acknowledge the influence of Western cultures, and I am interested in the other cultures of Asia and the cultures of African races and others. The idea of a pure racial culture in this era of cultural fusion is a slogan to cheat people, and nothing more than a myth.

It is the fate of the individual not to be able to attain ultimate truth, whether he calls it God, the other shore or the other side of death. The awareness that an individual is able to attain is what I call rationality, but it is not an ism.

Wilted Chrysanthemums

2 November 1991, Paris

KONG JIESHENG HAS SENT ME a letter suggesting that I write about my turbulent experiences in avant-garde theatre, from *Absolute Signal* and *Bus Stop* to *Wild Man*. Those were already wilted chrysanthemums and it seemed pointless to talk about them again, yet instantly the events of those years began to appear vividly before my eyes. At present those involved are still alive, and if someone were to write an account in the future there might be no one to verify what happened. So, rather than leave it as an unsettled case for the curious or the kind-hearted to waste their time on, it would be best for me to write my account. Moreover, I cannot be sure whether I will be interested in writing about these memories in future.

In June 1981 I was transferred through the Chinese Writers' Association to work as a writer at the People's Art Theatre in Beijing. Yu Shizhi, who was a Deputy Director of the Theatre, wanted me to write a play immediately. After I had discussed three of my ideas with him, he said that *Bus Stop* was the furthest from reality and the least likely to end up breaking any taboos.

In July, Ye Wenfu, Su Shuyang, Li Tuo and I enjoyed the privilege of spending a few days at Beidaihe as new members of the Chinese Writers' Association. During the day I would swim in the sea and work on *Bus Stop*, and at night I would drink alcohol and eat crab that I had bought and cooked myself. I also gave a talk on French surrealist poetry and avant-garde literature, and when Ye Wenfu immediately wrote "I Am a Zero" and Su Shuyang came forth with "Lust for Poetry Writing and Me", everyone shouted their approval.

It was a very happy time, but this ideal state of affairs was to last only a few days. Late one night the veteran writer Bai Hua suddenly arrived and told us that the highest authority in the Communist Party had singled him out for criticism. He also said that Ye Wenfu's poem about a certain general was about to bring disaster to Ye Wenfu, and soon a series of misfortunes did in fact befall him.

I completed *Bus Stop* a week after returning to Beijing. When the play director Lin Zhaohua read it he wanted to start rehearsals immediately, but Yu Shizhi had probably realised that the political climate was not right, so he urged us not to get ourselves involved in this sort of absurdist writing, and to stage a more realist play first.

Another Deputy Director of the People's Art Theatre, Xia Chun, introduced Lin Zhaohua and me to a young man called Liu Huiyuan, who told us about some railway law cases. I ended up paying a visit to the Beijing Railway Police Bureau to familiarise myself with some of the documents, and also travelled a few times with the guards on goods trains and prisoner trains. One weekend, from Saturday afternoon to early Monday morning, making use of two tape recorders — one to play and one to record — I wrote *Absolute Signal*, in thirty-six hours.

As long as it is not thought of as a movement, small theatre in fact began in China's largest theatre. Lin Zhaohua and I planned to break away from the established Stanislavsky patterns of realist theatre — in terms of both actor performance and the form of the production — but we kept this to ourselves and did not publicise it. We had the authorisation of the two Deputy Directors, Diao Guangtan and Yu Shizhi, and veteran actor Lin Liankun and the entire theatre group were highly cooperative at rehearsals. So from spring 1982, when we began to plan rehearsals, to summer, when we started to rehearse and make plans for the opening, we grew more and more confident.

During this period, Huang Weijing suggested that my essays on modern fiction, which had been serialised from 1980 in the Guangzhou magazine *Jottings* without attracting much attention, be published as a collection. *Preliminary Explorations into the Art of Modern Fiction* was published by Huacheng Publishing House in the autumn of 1981, and came to the notice of established writers. When Wang Meng read it he immediately said to Liu Xinwu: "This will cause a war at the gate of the Ministry of Culture." (At the time the Chinese Writers' Association was housed in the Ministry of Culture building complex.) His joke proved to be a correct prediction. In June 1982 he published an open letter addressed to me in *World of Fiction*. In his unique style of humour, not only did he express approval of my little book but he also suggested that I "continue exploring"! Next, Liu Xinwu also recommended the book in an article in *Reading*, and at the end of 1982 *Shanghai Literature* also published letters about the book by the writers Feng Jicai, Liu Xinwu and Li Tuo.

A pretext for making war on modernism had now been found, and the war began in *Literary Gazette*, the official publication of the Chinese Writers' Association. First, Feng Mu, the Party Secretary of the Writers' Association, said in a talk that some minor writer had written a ridiculous, reactionary little book that was having a harmful effect on new writers but had major writers applauding it. Realism was being seriously challenged, and this would have a bad effect on the direction of the nation's literature. Almost the whole of this lengthy talk appeared in an internal publication of the Writers' Association, one that was aimed specifically at the higher echelons, and immediately a response to the talk appeared in *Literary Gazette*, in the form of a letter from a reader. One after another of my friends in the Writers' Association relayed this to me, so I knew that this so-called letter from a reader had in fact come from the pen of the editor. The trumped-up charges being brought against Wang Meng in *Literary Gazette* right now are part of an attempt to start a campaign similar to the anti-Hu Feng and anti-rightist campaigns of earlier times. When the Party is in control of literature and the arts it can only end up like this.

Absolute Signal was staged in this sort of atmosphere. Few from the Party Committee and the Art Committee of the Theatre attended the dress rehearsal, and when the play ended, for a long time no one spoke. Finally Yu Shizhi uttered a few words: "It seems all right. Let's stage it and see what people think." I remain grateful for his support.

Originally two internal performances were scheduled and these were to be confined to people working in theatre circles. But by the night of the premiere, news had spread. In the rehearsal theatre where the performance was to take place, the seats were all filled and people were climbing up ladders that had not been removed and onto stage props. When the performance ended, people refused to leave and talked to the actors until one o'clock in the morning.

As it was experimental theatre, Lin Zhaohua was able to increase the number of performances to ten. At every performance the theatre was full to capacity and many of the audience stayed on and talked to the actors until late into the night. Large numbers of news items and reviews written by young journalists were also published.

The play was then performed for the public and created an instant sensation. The French magazine *Cosmopolitan* declared: "This play announces the birth of avant-garde theatre in Beijing." The Director of the Theatre, renowned playwright Cao Yu, sent a congratulatory telegram from Shanghai, and up to ten theatres throughout China fought to stage the play.

He Jingzhi, who was in charge of literature in the Ministry of Propaganda of the Chinese Communist Party Central Committee, found out about all this and promptly came to see the play. He had not realised the extent of its impact on audiences and it was awkward for him to do anything; it was not the right time, so he just made a few ambiguous remarks. For this reason, the controversy over the play focused on aesthetics and creative method and was confined to the theatre world, unlike the debate surrounding that little book of mine, which was already enmeshed in the politics of the literary world.

Not long afterwards, in his 1983 Spring Festival speech to the literary world, He Jingzhi publicly demanded the denunciation of modernism, and he coupled this with an attack on capitalist liberalisation, to give it added authority. The veteran writer Ye Junjian, who had written the preface for that little book of mine that had nothing to do with politics, told me that at an expanded Party meeting of the Writers' Association I had been named and criticised, and that repeated reference had also been made to Wang Meng. At that point I understood that I, being such a minor writer, was not the main target, and that struggles in the higher ranks of politics were being manifested in the literary world.

I was not willing to be a chess piece that was manipulated by others. I had to try to ward off the stick that was beating me. I wrote a letter to the writer Ba Jin and went to visit the playwright Xia Yan; both of them had shown concern for me in the past. At Xia Yan's place I saw Li Ziyun, who was in charge of *Shanghai Literature*. At the beginning of the year *Shanghai Literature* had published Ba Jin's conversation with a foreign journalist in two successive issues. He had notably talked about modernism as a literary school, and had said that if young people wanted to write in that style it was nothing to worry about. In a subsequent issue, Xia Yan had written a long article in which he even said that Lu Xun was a modernist.

Literary Gazette convened a conference on modernism which I was given notice to attend; the idea was to mobilise writers with different creative outlooks to criticise me. Unexpectedly, more than ten writers from Beijing refused to attack me, right to Feng Mu's face. Wang Meng was the first to retaliate. Then Cong Weixi said he had read my book and saw nothing wrong with it, and went on to declare that the stone engravings on the Han dynasty tomb of Huo Qubing were not realist. This attempt to incite Beijing writers to criticise me had failed.

Literary Gazette then went to Nanjing to mobilise the writers there, but encountered opposition at the meeting from magazines of Jiangsu Province such as *Bell Mountain*. The writer Chen Huangmei had not spoken at the Beijing meeting, but he went to Nanjing, and his speech on behalf of my book was subsequently published in the internal newsletter of the Nanjing-based publication *Youth*. At a conference on theory held by the Ministry of Propaganda at Tongxian, on the outskirts of Beijing, the late Zhong Dianfei, from the Literature Research Institute of the Chinese Academy of Social Sciences, prevailed over dissenters and spoke with great feeling in defence of my book. Several veteran writers such as Yan Wenjing and Feng Yidai also spoke on my behalf; Li Shifei, the editor of Huacheng Publishing House, deflected a lot of pressure from me too. After spring 1983 the political climate relaxed, so for the time being I avoided the stick that was being wielded above my head.

In April and May of 1983, Lin Zhaohua and I had again begun making plans to rehearse *Bus Stop*. I should mention that the Party Committee of the People's Art Theatre had not given its approval for this play. Cao Yu, the veteran Director of the Theatre, was sick and in hospital, so we went to visit him. When we told him about the play, he said: "It's a global subject, why can't you stage it?" Having heard these words of his, we found a few enthusiastic actors to do some internal actor training, and rehearsed behind closed doors. (Luckily, most of the hundred or so actors of the Theatre had nothing to do, because for years there had been no plays to perform.)

The play had been fully rehearsed by July, the height of summer. Before the dress rehearsal I went to Cao Yu's place, and we ate and drank till very late. He was completely open with me despite my being of a younger generation; he even showed me a letter from the artist Huang Yongyu, criticising him for not having written any good plays since 1949. I was genuinely fond of the old man and felt that there were no barriers between us. Cao Yu, who had never taken part in deciding which plays were to be staged at the Theatre, turned up for the dress rehearsal with his walking stick, accompanied by his youngest daughter. When the play ended, of course, no one spoke. Few in the theatre were willing to play the role of judge, and only he, holding his walking stick high in the air, shouted: "Bravo!"

This closed experimental performance took place in the banquet hall on the third floor of the Capital Theatre, with all the windows covered in black cloth. Chairs were arranged around all four sides of the hall and the performance took place in the middle of the audience. There were seats for more than two hundred; every seat was taken and people were standing. It was a two-hour performance, in a space that had no ventilation, and it was unbearably hot. Not a single person walked out, and there was laughter and clapping from beginning to end. At the end, a large part of the audience refused to leave and talked to theatre personnel on the balcony late into the night. It was like this for each of the ten performances.

We did not invite any journalists, but news leaked out, and Feng Mu suddenly arrived to see the play. When it ended, I asked him what he thought of it, but he left without a word. Despite the enthusiasm of the audience, those of us in the theatre were very anxious. There were no further performances.

Late one night, Su Shuyang came especially to inform me that someone had just told him about He Jingzhi's pronouncement on *Bus Stop*: "The play is more *Hai Rui is*

Dismissed from Office than *Hai Rui is Dismissed from Office*. It is the most poisonous play written since the founding of the People's Republic of China." He Jingzhi had not seen the play, but had obviously heard reports. Su Shuyang, who was sweating profusely on my behalf, urged me to pay He Jingzhi a visit to explain things. I merely replied that I knew the man. I also knew that I had managed to get away once, but that I would not be able to get away a second time. So I simply went off to have a good time on the coast at Xingcheng, where *People's Literature* had organised a get-together for new writers.

I had never felt so free and relaxed. I took swimming lessons, dug up razor clams on the beach or just looked out at the sea, but I did not write a word. At night I swam in the sea, or danced. (It was through an editor of *People's Literature*, Wang Nanning, that I learned most of my dance repertoire.)

After the whole *Bus Stop* affair had ended, Xu Gang told me that everyone had been worried about my being in a comatose state and were afraid that I might attempt suicide. This was because an assistant editor had just been to a meeting of the Writers' Association in Dalian at which Feng Mu had singled me out as having a very serious problem. But none of my friends had dared tell me at the time. It was no wonder that whenever I went into the sea at night, Wang Nanning and a young writer from Yunnan stayed close to me, one in front of me and one behind. Both of them were excellent swimmers, so I did not need to worry about swimming a long way out.

When I returned to Beijing, the situation was already very tense. It just so happened that I had returned in time for the routine health examinations at the Theatre, and they found a shadow on my lungs. I took sick leave and fled south to stay with my younger brother. At a second examination, at a hospital, they again gave a wrong diagnosis of lung cancer. In the interim, people wrote from Beijing telling me that the Ministry of Propaganda had ordered the Theatre to stage two performances of *Bus Stop*, and had issued the tickets to specific work units so they could write criticisms.

Meanwhile, taking advantage of Hu Yaobang's visit to Japan, the Oppose Spiritual Pollution Campaign was unleashed throughout the country. On television a flurry of leading personalities, from all levels of political and cultural life in Beijing and the provincial capitals, came forward to state their positions. But I felt that all this was of no relevance to me. My father had died of lung cancer, within just three months of being diagnosed. Since it seemed that I did not have many days left, I started roaming the free markets buying fresh fish, prawns and crabs, which were normally not available in Beijing, then cooking and eating them. When I was not doing that, I read *The Book of Changes*.

However, a couple of weeks later, when I went to the hospital for a further examination by a specialist, the shadow on my lung had miraculously vanished.

I had won a reprieve from death, but I still had to comply with an order to return to Beijing. When I got back, a so-called journalist from *Literary Gazette* came to the Theatre several times wanting to see me, but I refused on the ground of illness. However, the man went to the extent of waiting outside the door of the playwrights' office, where he eventually bailed me up. He said he only wanted a few words, but of course I knew what that meant.

I had been inside attending a meeting, because instructions from the higher echelons required each of the writers at the Theatre to state his position on "eradicating spiritual pollution". None of the other writers had mentioned my play. Then it was my turn to speak. I must admit, at the time I was a nervous wreck. I suddenly lost control, smashed the cup I was holding to pieces, swore, got up and left. It was then that I ran into the journalist waiting outside the door. Afterwards, everyone settled me into bed, but I was still highly agitated.

It was the Theatre that protected me. Hu Qiaomu, the committee member in charge of ideology at the Political Bureau, had already written directly to Yu Shizhi, saying in a congenial tone that People's Art in Beijing was a theatre with an international reputation and that it should uphold the path of realism. However, working through the Ministry of Propaganda, He Jingzhi issued orders to *Literary Gazette*, *Drama Magazine* and *Beijing Daily*, as well as *October* magazine, which had published *Bus Stop*, to arrange for articles that would denounce the play; he said that the sort of person who would write such a play should be sent to Qinghai for training. During the late 1950s some friends of mine were branded rightists and sent for reform-through-labour to Qinghai, and only one in ten had survived. (Back in those days, they did not go as reform-through-labour prisoners; the euphemism of "going for training" was used instead.)

It seemed best for me to run away in advance, so as to avoid not being able to get away when the time came. I left the Theatre with a document stating that I was going to the forests in the highlands of the great southwest to get first-hand experience of the lives of the woodcutters there, so that if the authorities made inquiries it would be easier for the Theatre. I had no time to wait for a travel allowance, but I took with me the four-hundred-*yuan* advance royalty that I had received from the People's Literature Publishing House for my novel *Soul Mountain*. As soon as my feet touched the ground in Chengdu, I made my way into the primeval forests of the giant panda reserve in northwest Sichuan.

During the Cultural Revolution, while I was at cadre school, the army representative had put me before a study group to undergo criticism and I had run away. I had thrown away my Beijing residential permit and settled for five years in a farm village in the mountain regions of southern Anhui Province.

Fleeing, I think, is the most reliable strategy for the protection of the self. From the huge snow-clad mountains of Sichuan, I travelled eastwards to the coast. I visited eight provinces and seven nature reserves in my fifteen-thousand-kilometre journey of wandering, which lasted five months. No one was able to find me, yet I had friends who would pass on news from Beijing whenever I stopped for a while. Local friends told me I had been named in internal Party documents on the Oppose Spiritual Pollution Campaign that were being circulated in the counties.

During this five-month period Hu Yaobang gradually strengthened his position and the Oppose Spiritual Pollution Campaign began to peter out. However, for some reason He Jingzhi simply refused to let me off. But an article attacking me in *Literary Gazette* that he had "personally drafted" angered another committee member of the Political Bureau, Duan Junyi, then First Secretary of the Beijing Municipal Committee, who issued a counter-criticism document in which criticisms of me were designated as "internal contradictions of the people". The Propaganda Department of the Municipal Committee therefore deleted a third of He Jingzhi's article, which had been forwarded to them by the Central Propaganda Department, and sent it back with all of the most serious political judgments crossed out. *Beijing Daily* and *October* have never published an article criticising *Bus Stop*; the only public criticisms appeared in *Literary Gazette* and *Theatre Magazine*, both of which are directly controlled by the Ministry of Propaganda of the Central Committee.

A theatre company in Yugoslavia joined in the excitement and wanted to stage *Bus Stop* on 1 October 1984, during China's National Day celebrations. The Chinese Writers' Association cabled the Chinese Embassy there to "dissuade our Yugoslav friends". However, the theatre company was not dissuaded. The play was staged as scheduled, and was even broadcast on Hungarian National Radio.

So I went back to Beijing feeling relaxed. Wang Meng, the Chief Editor of *People's Literature*, authorised the release of my short story "Hua Dou". It had been shelved and effectively banned for more than a year, and thereafter it was possible to publish manuscripts of mine that had been shelved with other magazines. Following this, China Theatre Publishing House published my book *Artistic Explorations in "Absolute Signal"*, and Beijing Publishing House released my novella *A Pigeon Called Red Beak*, though without the preface Feng Yidai had written for it. Yu Haocheng, the Director of The Masses Publishing House, sent an editor to see me and then published a collection of eight of my plays, for which the renowned playwright Wu Zuguang wrote a very detailed preface. Unfortunately, later on, during the Oppose Capitalist Liberalisation Campaign, this book became one of the criminal charges leading to Yu Haocheng's dismissal.

Wild Man was written during the congenial climate following Hu Yaobang's suppression of the Oppose Spiritual Pollution Campaign. At Yu Shizhi's suggestion, I completed this play in ten days and ten nights during November 1984. Lin Zhaohua and I had talked about establishing a form of modern Eastern theatre that would be unlike the normal form of Western spoken drama. That was the general conclusion to the first stage of our theatre experimentations: our plan was to make total theatre. At the beginning of 1985 we started training actors, and exploring various modes of stage performance. We also invited Yin Guangzhong from Guizhou to come to Beijing to make the masks for the production.

During this period the Fourth National Representative Congress of the Writers' Association was convened, and for the first time many new and younger writers were able to attend, but my name was not on the list. Liu Binyan argued and managed to get invitations for both Zhang Xinxin and me to a meeting of the Secretariat of the Writers' Association. After that there was the Fourth National Representative Congress of the Drama Association, and again my name was not on the list. Wu Zuguang nominated me time and again, but without success. So, in accepting his invitation to the preparatory meeting of the Chairman's Group, he wrote on the back of it that if there were in fact not enough places at the Congress, he would give his to Gao Xingjian, and he himself would not attend. The day before the Congress was to begin, the Drama Association telephoned the People's Art Theatre to advise them that I could attend as a specially invited representative. Both these events amounted to coercing the Writers' Association and the Drama Association into overturning their respective verdicts on my case.

The dress rehearsal for *Wild Man* was held at the end of April 1985 and the play was publicly performed at the beginning of May, this time in the main auditorium of the Capital Theatre. Cao Yu had seen the dress rehearsal, and he said to me: "Young Gao, you've come up with another kind of theatre." This greatly moved me.

For the opening night we had invited people from the literary and art world, actors and journalists from various newspapers. Yi Wensi came with his wife, and afterwards, when he went onstage to congratulate the actors, he was so excited that he wept. Then, turning to me, he said in front of the audience: "You have already achieved on stage what I have been trying to realise in film." The review of the play in the *Christian Science Monitor* in the United States included the words "truly amazing".

In China the play again caused controversy in theatre circles, but this time it was purely on artistic grounds and politics was not brought into it. However, in the same year, when the Ministry of Culture was compiling a list of the finest plays over the past few years and the selection committee unanimously selected *Absolute Signal* for the top position, a notification from above said that the play was not eligible for selection. Wu Zuguang was furious and resigned from the selection committee.

In May, I went by invitation to Berlin as part of the Culture and Arts Exchange Program of the Federal Republic of Germany. In addition, the French Ministry of Foreign Affairs and Ministry of Culture invited me twice to France, where a symposium on my plays was held in Paris at the National Theatre of the People. A number of universities in Europe also held symposiums and conferences on my works.

I returned to Beijing at the beginning of 1986 and wrote a new play, *The Other Shore*. Lin Zhaohua and I used the People's Art Theatre trainee class for rehearsals, but these were stopped after only a month. We then planned to establish an experimental theatre workshop, but that did not happen either.

The Oppose Capitalist Liberalisation Campaign had finally toppled the enlightened Hu Yaobang. Yet the old leftists within the Party refused to stop at that point, and persisted until they had also purged Zhao Ziyang in June 1989 and openly fired on students in a massacre.

At the end of 1987, when I travelled abroad once more in response to an invitation, I already had a premonition that it would be impossible for my plays to be staged in China again. The political authorities there would only approve plays that would serve as tools of propaganda for them, so what art was there to speak of?

In 1986 the Swedish Royal Theatre performed my play "Getting Out of the Rain" from *Highlights of Modern Opera*, and in 1987 the Hong Kong Dance Company performed another new play of mine, *Netherworld*, then in 1988 the Thalia Theatre of Hamburg invited Lin Zhaohua to direct

Wild Man. In 1990 the Wiener Unterhaltungs Theater performed *Bus Stop* in a newly built subway station that was not yet in use, the Taiwan National Art Academy performed *The Other Shore*, and Panther Theatre in Hong Kong performed *Wild Man.* In March 1992 the Swedish Royal Theatre will stage *Fleeing*, a play that was reprinted as a reactionary work in China and made me a target for attack. My most recent play, *Between Life and Death*, was commissioned by the French Ministry of Culture; a subsidy has been received and preparations are underway for a production.

My old accounts have been settled and my experiments in theatre are about to start a new phase.

Another Kind of Theatre

1 February 1993, Paris

IS THERE ANOTHER KIND OF THEATRE in between traditional Chinese opera and Western spoken drama? Or to put it another way, is there another kind of theatre apart from the two major types of drama — Asian theatre, in which the singing and dancing of professionals is primary (as in Chinese opera, Japanese Noh and Kabuki, and Indonesia's Balinese dance opera), and European theatre, in which the playwright's lines are primary?

The answer is, of course, yes. Western opera, dance drama and mime, and Eastern storytelling, singing with stringed instruments, shadow play, puppet theatre, and even dancing monkeys and stalls selling dog-skin plaster can all count as theatre. My various experiments in theatre are efforts to completely destroy the barriers between all of these and to modify and adapt each of them for my own use.

The rise of the institution of directors in modern Western theatre since the end of the last century has led to endless revolutions in the ancient art of theatre. New concepts, new performance methods and new stage techniques have emerged in an endless stream, and there are now more ideologies and schools than can be counted. So instead of trying to catch up to or repeat what others have done, I think it best to find my own path.

Western critics have called my plays avant-garde, but in China they have been called absurdist, sometimes nativist, and they have also been classed as postmodernist. I prefer not to be placed in any category and thus hope to avoid wrapping myself in a cocoon. Altogether, I have written fifteen plays of varying length, and the language and modes of expression are quite different in each. Some resemble the words sung in traditional Chinese opera; some have choruses as in opera; some are long soliloquies from beginning to end; and some contain characters that do not speak. I have included peasant work songs, asides, narration and polyphony, and I have made use of modern dance and mime-style performance. My plays feature tragedy, comedy, farce and tragicomedy, as well the simultaneous use of both absurdism and realism. I have used the classical Western three unities principle and approximations of the prose essay form quite freely throughout an entire work. As for the language used in my plays, there is both modern and classical Chinese, and the dialects of Beijing and other regions; there is Chinese, broken English, and also French language games, because at times I also write in French. I think even poetry and the prose essay may be imported into plays, but naturally on the condition that they comply with the principles of theatre, and that they be constructed as theatre.

I do not wish to apply to myself the label of any style or group, but I do have my own ideas about what constitutes theatre. Although I make use of all sorts of techniques, I place absolute importance on the structural integrity of a play. Whether a play can be staged depends primarily on its structure. Theatre is action, but sadly many modern playwrights have forgotten this irrefutable principle. Often what is written is careless and uninteresting — endless empty prattle, even psychological or semantic analysis — and the resulting play is tired and listless. It is therefore not surprising that the art of the director has gradually replaced the art of theatre. In this era of the dictatorship of the director, regaining a place for the play in theatre requires playwrights to rethink what in fact constitutes theatre.

The proposal that theatre is a process, first made by the French dramatic theorist Artaud and reinforced by performances of plays written by the Polish playwright Kantor, revived the age-old concept of action in theatre. This greatly enlightened me. In addition, I discovered that theatre could be change, theatre could be contrast, and that theatre could be discovery and surprise. Theatricality therefore lies precisely in the action, sequence of events, change, contrast, discovery and surprise that are inherent in the structure of a play. All of my plays are so structured, and this may be considered the crux of my idea of theatre.

I believe that in the final analysis the art of theatre must depend on the actualisation of the actor's performance on stage. So, in order to realise all of my ideas about plays, I had to extend my research on actor performance. I observed and analysed the performances of actors in traditional Chinese opera, and from this I discovered that Western performance theories have only ever talked about a twofold relationship: that of the actor to the role. What had been overlooked was the stage of transition from the living person who will act to the role he will act, which I denote as the state of the "neutral actor". By this I mean that prior to the actor's entering his role, he must cleanse himself of the individual he is in normal life. If theatre performance establishes this interval and fully indicates this process, then managing the threefold relationship between self, actor and role can provide many new possibilities in performance art and also enrich the writing of plays. My tripartite theory of performance is manifested in many of my works, and is often the turning point in my plays.

This sort of performance theory emphasises the actor's performance before an audience. A high level of theatricality is a feature of my plays, because I believe that this is what differentiates theatre from visual arts such as film and television. When sound, light and colour flood a modern theatre through various technical means, the artistic installation created on the stage is manipulated by the director so that it often simply turns the actor into a living object to be placed in a certain position. I prefer to return to the performance of the actor himself. Moreover, I believe that the versatility of an actor's performance is the soul of theatre.

Because of this, I advocate returning to a bare stage, and reducing scenery to a minimum. *Bus Stop* was performed in Vienna in a newly built subway station that was not yet in use, and the subway entrance and the empty thirty- to forty-metre platform constituted the performance space. When I directed *Dialogue and Rebuttal*, the whole theatre, even the stage and audience seats, was completely white, so that it was possible for the audience to see every expression of the actors' eyes.

A stage prop, on the other hand, can turn into a live object. The performance of an actor can bestow it with life, so that it becomes a character with whom the other characters can interact. For instance, a wooden fish on the stage can be envisaged as a human head. In my play *Between Life and Death*, a leg and a hand hanging in midair materialise as projections of the female protagonist's self. The cardboard house that she takes out of a suitcase evokes a string of childhood memories. When the cardboard house collapses, she returns to reality. As objects on the stage come to life through an actor's performance, the unlimited imagination of the audience is activated, and the space of the performance is longer limited to the stage. The varied use of props and stage settings is likewise an integral part of the composition of my plays.

My plays have been staged in Europe mostly with Western directors, but at times I have personally directed them. My collaboration with Western directors and actors has been a very happy one. Communicating these ideas of mine to them was not at all difficult, and the actors also became familiar with them after a while. Individual directors work in different ways, and although I exchange views with them, I never interfere.

Between Life and Death, directed by Alain Timar in Paris, and Nürnberg City Theatre's production of *Fleeing* in Germany were unlike anything I had expected, but both were superb. In the case of the production of *Fleeing* by the Swedish Royal Theatre, I was invited for discussions with the director and choreographer prior to rehearsals, and was allowed to give some training to the actors; this was yet another way of working. When the Thalia Theatre in Hamburg staged *Wild Man*, my old friend Lin Zhaohua was invited to come and direct it. As for plays I have directed myself — rehearsing with German-speaking actors for *Dialogue and Rebuttal* in Austria and with English-speaking actors for *Between Life and Death* in Australia — I was able to decide on the actors and to fully experiment with my own methods. I believe that the same play may be interpreted in very different ways. What is important is that it be produced, and that it be produced well.

In modern times the avant-garde theatre of the West has gone through an anti-theatre phase that was initiated by playwrights. Yet *Waiting for Godot* and *The Bald Soprano* in the late 1950s were successful because of the writing, and they are plays that can still be performed today. By the 1960s and 1970s, following the rise of the director-oriented play, the status of drama on stage gradually declined, and while there have been many superb productions, few plays of that era will survive to see future performances.

By the end of the 1980s the various experiments of the directors had gone full circle, and it was found that while sound, lighting, colour, performance setting and expression using the arms and legs were interesting, the most interesting thing after all was language. So there was a return to traditional theatre, a search for scripts that had been discarded, and a rush to present new interpretations of classical plays. The result was that Greek tragedy, Shakespeare and Chekhov again became popular.

Then what about contemporary plays? At this point the deceased German-language playwright Thomas Bernhard, whose plays were banned in his homeland of Austria during his lifetime, was discovered. The French playwright Bernard-Marie Koltes was also dead; when he was alive only six of his plays had been performed, and had drawn little response. England's Ezra Pound was still alive, but he was already over sixty.

The conclusion, then, is not to go chasing fashions, because fashions will always become outdated. Today's are right and yesterday's are wrong, and tomorrow they will be wilted chrysanthemums. This is the meaning of fashion. In writing plays I follow the path of my own thinking, and when I have an idea I try to develop it, rather than simply chasing after new forms and fashionable trends. My play *Bus Stop* is a lyrical comedy about real life; it is neither speculative nor anti-theatre.

I do not discuss philosophy in my plays; the circumstances of human existence can indeed give rise to all sorts of philosophical speculation, but it is existence itself that has the greatest authenticity. This is so in art and it is so in theatre. I am not against realism but I am against the idea of imposing its tenets on artistic creation. Although I do not subscribe to realism, this does not mean that I avoid social reality. My plays *Absolute Signal*, *Bus Stop*, *Wild Man* and *Fleeing* are all concerned with this reality, but they are not satisfied with simply revealing scenes of real life, because the perceptions of people's minds are equally real. I think highly of Chekhov and Genet because I encounter genuine feelings in their work. Genet's plays may be grotesque, but in his eyes reality often revealed itself that way; his plays do not try to analyse this reality intellectually, but they are infused with psychological and perceptual truth. I do not treat reality and absurdity as opposites; I regard both as similarly valid. Absurdity is concealed in real life, and in my plays I often unveil it progressively, so my plays are realist and absurdist at the same time, and it is hard for me to place myself in any school. But regardless of what method is used to write a play, in my view it is always a feeling of authenticity that gives life to a work of art.

I have also written a cycle of plays as part of my research on performance methodology: *Soliloquy*, *Modern Highlights from Opera* (in four parts) and *The Other Shore*. It could be said that I wrote them specifically for actors, but they are also interesting for general audiences. It is not necessary to produce a staged recreation of the illusion of life in order to evoke a sense of reality. I emphasise that it is theatre that the audience comes to the theatre to see. The feeling of truth in a performance lies firstly in the actor's conviction, and secondly in his convincing the audience through the art of his performance. This cycle of plays has not been performed in the West, and although actors from Germany, Sweden and France have made inquiries about *Soliloquy*, and some have even purchased the performance rights, it still has not gone on stage. These plays have performance methods that are very different from the accepted methods of the West and it is probably difficult to know how to begin. It is only the Swedish Royal Theatre that has performed "Getting Out of the Rain", one of the four parts of *Modern Highlights from Opera*, and the performance successfully conveyed the poetry of performance art. Taiwan National Art Academy has performed *The Other Shore*, but unfortunately I was not able to see it.

Netherworld and *Romance of "The Classic of Mountains and Seas"* may be said to have concluded my research on actor performance, at times carried out on traditional Chinese opera and at times on myths from China's antiquity. The former play adapts material from the traditional opera *Smashing Open the Coffin* and focuses on Hell, while the latter is a textual study of *The Classic of Mountains and Seas* and deals with more than seventy deities, from Nüwa, who created humans, to Yu the

Great, who unified the empire. These plays give a clue as to what I mean by "another kind of theatre". They are neither traditional Chinese opera nor spoken drama, contain dance and music yet are not song-and-dance theatre, and make use of vaudeville and smoke and fire, storytelling and sorcerers' dances, and even symphonic choruses. This kind of theatre is naturally difficult for Westerners, and only the Hong Kong Dance Group has performed a dance version of *Netherworld*, with Jiang Qing as director.

Over the past three years I have written three plays: *Between Life and Death*, *Dialogue and Rebuttal* and *Nocturnal Wanderer*. They tell of life and death, and the possibility that what lies between reality and subjective thinking is just a nightmare; they all depict people's inner worlds. In these plays the connection with reality is a pretext, because what I sought to capture was the reality of psychological perceptions. This naked reality has no need to conceal anything; it is greater than religious, ethical or philosophical explanations of it and transcends all ideologies, and through it humans are more human, and more fully manifest the original likeness of humans. When *Between Life and Death* was performed in Paris, newspaper reviewers wrote that the play had created "a prototype woman", so in my new play *Nocturnal Wanderer* I set out to produce a prototype man or person. *Dialogue and Rebuttal* borrows the reply mode of Chan Buddhist *gong'an*, and raises questions about language. Can language fully articulate human existence? Behind language games, could it be that the unknowable is in fact human nature, and is it that language fabrications are in fact human fabrications?

My investigations into theatrical form have always aimed at allowing me to display as far as possible the stark naked truth of the circumstances of modern human existence. If a dramatic form does not come closer to this truth, but instead buries it, then the form is dubious and can turn into a little tactic, a little trick, a little decoration or a little toy for winning notoriety and popularity.

Revolutionising form should not become a sort of superstition. Is there any certainty that what comes later will be able to negate what came earlier? The idea that only the new is good has become the disease of our times, and probably has become the collective subconscious of consumerist society. But art is not merchandise, and for the artist, being able to reject market forces is critical to his being able to write good works, because these forces exert pressures harder to resist than politics or social customs. Over the past century, theatre, and more generally literature and the arts, have come full circle, from searching for form back to focusing on human existence, on which they rely for expression and from which they obtain expression, so they have not moved forward much.

These plays of mine propose nothing more than a return to the source of theatre, a restoration of the rationale for the existence of this art form. I believe that although my experimentation in writing plays has not been able to realise everything I wanted to, they have nevertheless led to quite a number of plays, so I can now come to a temporary stop, because I should certainly do some other things.

The Necessity of Loneliness

Speech presented on receiving the Golden Plate Award at the Forty-first International Achievement Summit of the American Academy of Achievement, held on 8 June 2002 in Dublin. Published in the Literary Supplement of the Taiwanese daily Lianhebao, *11 July 2002*

THE FEELING OF LONELINESS IS unique to humans. A tree or a bird may seem to be lonely, but this is an attribute bestowed by the person making the observation. The tree or the bird is incapable of perceiving loneliness. This feeling occurs when a person is alone, and, moved by his emotions, associates his own circumstances with those of the bird or the tree that he sees before him. Since this feeling entails an element of self-examination, it is not a purely objective observation. The feeling of loneliness produced is thus a form of aesthetics, in that while observing one's external environment, one is at the same time examining the self that is located within it, and to a certain extent this is an affirmation of one's own personal worth.

This feeling of loneliness, which stems from self-love, can arouse self-pity or lead to conceitedness, and can even turn into unbridled impetuousness. If concern for the external world is lost, this feeling can become a tangled mass in the heart and turn into an affliction that gives rise to arrogance and bigotry.

To derive interest from loneliness instead of allowing it to become an affliction, one must examine both what is external and what is internal — in other words, use another eye to calmly observe the outside world as well as one's own inner world. This third eye, which can transcend the limitations of one's self, is what is known as consciousness, or even wisdom.

However, wisdom or consciousness comes also with distance — in other words, with taking a step back. One requires a certain distance to be able to see clearly and make accurate judgments about people and events.

Loneliness is not merely an aesthetic judgment, because it can also turn into a drive. Since it is premised on affirming an individual's worth, it contributes to motivating the individual to go forth and overcome difficulties, or pursue a particular goal.

It is only when a child is alone that he starts to become an adult, and it is only when a person is alone that he can achieve maturity. Loneliness is essential for adults. It encourages independence, and needless to say, the ability to endure loneliness is indispensable for strengthening character within social situations.

It is bad not to have this vital distance between the individual and others, to be running into people all the time — either within a family or within some other collective unit. Moreover, coexistence requires magnanimity and understanding, and these depend on our having adequate space between ourselves and others.

To an even greater extent, loneliness is a prerequisite for freedom. Freedom depends on the ability to reflect, and reflection can only begin when one is alone.

The world does not consist only of dualities — right or wrong, condoning or opposing, revolutionary or reactionary, progressive or conservative, politically correct or politically incorrect. Before making a choice, there is no harm in hesitating and leaving a little room for independent reflection.

When ideologies, trends in thinking, fashions or crazes are all-embracing, it is being lonely that affirms the individual's freedom.

In the bustling world of today the propaganda of the mass media is all-pervasive, and if at times an individual wants to listen to the voice of his heart he will need the support of this feeling of loneliness. As long as it does not turn into an ailment, loneliness is necessary for the individual to establish himself and to achieve things.

I thank all of you here today at this illustrious gathering for patiently listening to me talk about insights that I have gained from my experiences. I am sure that all of you too have had such insights.

Appendix

Chronology of Gao Xingjian's major publications

"Hanye de xingchen", *Huacheng* 2 (1980).

"Xiandai xiaoshuo jiqiao chutan", serialised monthly in *Suibi* (1980).

"Falanxi xiandai wenxue de tongku", *Waiguo wenxue yanjiu* 1 (1980).

"Faguo xiandaipai renmin shiren Pulieweier he tade *Geci ji*",
　　Huacheng 5 (1980).

Xiandai xiaoshuo jiqiao chutan (Huacheng, Guangzhou, 1981;
　　reprinted 1982).

Juedui xinhao, *Shiyue* 5 (1982); reprinted in *Gao Xingjian xiju ji*
　　(1985); translated by Shiao-Ling S. Yu as *Alarm Signal* in *Chinese
　　Drama After the Cultural Revolution, 1979–1989*, edited by Shiao-
　　Ling S. Yu (Edwin Mellen, Lewiston, New York, 1996).

Chezhan, *Shiyue* 3 (Beijing, 1983); reprinted in *Gao Xingjian xiju ji*
　　(1985); translated by Shiao-Ling S. Yu as *The Bus Stop* in *Chinese
　　Drama After the Cultural Revolution, 1979–1989* (1996); also
　　translated by Kimberley Besio as *Bus Stop* in "*Bus Stop*: A Lyrical
　　Comedy on Life in One Act", in *Theater and Society: An Anthology
　　of Contemporary Chinese Drama*, edited by Haiping Yan (M. E.
　　Sharpe, Armonk, New York, 1998).

"Yuan'en si", *Haiyan* 8 (1983); translated by Mabel Lee as "The
　　Temple" in *Buying a Fishing Rod for My Grandfather* (2004).

"Gongyuan li", *Nanfang wenxue* 4 (1983); translated by Mabel Lee as
　　"In the Park" in *Buying a Fishing Rod for My Grandfather* (2004).

"Meng bo", *Huacheng* 3 (1983); translated by Mabel Lee as "Dream
　　Waves" in *A Birthday Book for Brother Stone: For David Hawkes, at
　　Eighty*, edited by Rachael May and John Minford (Chinese
　　University Press, Hong Kong, 2003).

"Choujin", *Xiaoshuo zhoubao* 1 (1984); translated by Mabel Lee as
　　"Cramp" in *Buying a Fishing Rod for My Grandfather* (2004).

"Pulieweier, *Geci ji*" (a translation of Jacques Prévert's *Paroles*), in
　　Waiguo xiandai shi, edited by Zheng Kelu (Renmin Wenxue,
　　Beijing, 1984) (two volumes).

You zhi gezi jiao Hongchunr (Shiyue Wenyi, Beijing, 1984).

"Younaisiku, *Tutou genü*" (a translation of Eugene Ionesco's *La Cantatrice Chauve*), in *Huangdanpai xiju*, edited by Chen Jialin (Renmin Wenxue, Beijing, 1985).

Gao Xingjian xiju ji (Qunzhong, Beijing, 1985).

Dubai, Shiye 2 (1985).

"Chehuo", *Fujian wenxue* 5 (1985); translated by Mabel Lee as "The Accident" in *Buying a Fishing Rod for My Grandfather* (2004).

Yeren, Shiye 2 (1985); reprinted in *Gao Xingjian xiju ji* (1985); translated by Bruno Roubicek as *Wild Man* in "*Wild Man*: A Contemporary Chinese Spoken Drama", *Asian Theatre Journal* 7.2 (Fall 1990).

"Gei wo laoye mai yugan", *Renmin wenxue* 9 (1986); reprinted in Gao Xingjian, *Gei wo laoye mai yugan* (1988); translated by Mabel Lee as "Buying a Fishing Rod for My Grandfather" in *Buying a Fishing Rod for My Grandfather* (2004).

Bi'an, Shiye 5 (1986); reprinted in *Gao Xingjian xiju liuzhong* (1995); translated by Jo Riley as *The Other Side* in "*The Other Side*: A Contemporary Drama Without Acts", in *An Oxford Anthology of Contemporary Chinese Drama*, edited by Martha P. Y. Cheung and Jane C. C. Lai (Hong Kong University Press, Oxford and New York, 1997); also translated by Gilbert C. F. Fong as *The Other Shore* in *The Other Shore: Plays by Gao Xingjian* (1999).

Dui yizhong xiandai xiju de zhuiqiu (Zhongguo Xiju, Beijing, 1988).

Gei wo laoye mai yugan (Lianhe Wenxue, Taipei, 1988); expanded as *Gao Xingjian duanpian xiaoshuo ji* (Lianhe Wenxue, Taipei, 2001); six stories of the latter edition translated by Mabel Lee in *Buying a Fishing Rod for My Grandfather* (2004).

Lingshan (Lianjing, Taipei, 1990); translated by Mabel Lee as *Soul Mountain* (2000).

Taowang, Jintian 1 (1990); reprinted in *Gao Xingjian xiju liuzhong* (1995); translated by Gregory B. Lee as *Fugitives* in *Chinese Writing and Exile*, edited by Gregory B. Lee (Center for East Asian Studies, University of Chicago, Chicago, 1993).

"Wo zhuzhang yizhong leng de wenxue", *Zhongshi wanbao* Literature Supplement (12 August 1990); reprinted in *Meiyou zhuyi* (1996); translated by Mabel Lee as "Cold Literature" in *Cold Literature: Selected Works by Gao Xingjian* (2005), and in *The Case for Literature* (2006).

"Guanyu *Taowang*", *Lianhebao* Literary Supplement (17 June 1991);
   reprinted in *Meiyou zhuyi* (1996); translated by Mabel Lee as
   "About *Fleeing*" in *The Case for Literature* (2006).

"Shunjian", *Zhongshi wanbao* Literature Supplement (1 September
   1991); reprinted in *Zhoumo sichongzhou* (1996); translated by
   Mabel Lee as "In an Instant" in *Buying a Fishing Rod for My
   Grandfather* (2004).

"Bali suibi", *Guangchang* 4 (1991); reprinted in *Meiyou zhuyi* (1996);
   translated by Gilbert C. F. Fong as "Parisian Notes" in *Cold
   Literature: Selected Works by Gao Xingjian* (2005).

Sheng si jie, *Jintian* 1 (1991); reprinted in *Gao Xingjian xiju liuzhong*
   (1995); translated by Gilbert C. F. Fong as *Between Life and Death*
   in *The Other Shore: Plays by Gao Xingjian* (1999).

"Wenxue yu xuanxue: Guanyu *Lingshan*", *Jintian* 3 (1992); reprinted
   in *Meiyou zhuyi* (1996); translated by Mabel Lee as "Literature and
   Metaphysics: About *Soul Mountain*" in *The Case for Literature*
   (2006).

"Geri huanghua", *Minzhu Zhongguo* 8 (1992); reprinted in *Meiyou
   zhuyi* (1996); translated by Mabel Lee as "Wilted
   Chrysanthemums" in *The Case for Literature* (2006).

Shanhaijing zhuan (Cosmos, Hong Kong, 1993); reprinted in *Gao
   Xingjian xiju liuzhong* (1995).

Au Bord de la Vie (Lansman, Carnières-Morlanwelz, 1993).

Duihua yu fanjie, *Jintian* 2 (1993); reprinted in *Gao Xingjian xiju
   liuzhong* (1995); translated by Gilbert C. F. Fong as *Dialogue and
   Rebuttal* in *The Other Shore: Plays by Gao Xingjian* (1999).

"Ling yizhong xiju" (1993), in *Meiyou zhuyi* (1996); translated by
   Mabel Lee as "Another Kind of Theatre" in *The Case for
   Literature* (2006).

"Geren de shengyin", *Mingbao yuekan* 8 (1993); collected in *Meiyou
   zhuyi* (1996); translated by Lena Aspfors and Torbjörn Lodén as
   "The Voice of the Individual", *The Stockholm Journal of East Asian
   Studies* 6 (1995); also translated by Mabel Lee as "The Voice of the
   Individual" in *The Case for Literature* (2006).

"Meiyou zhuyi" (1993), in *Meiyou zhuyi* (1996); translated by Winnie
   Lau, Deborah Sauviat and Martin Williams as "Without Isms",
   The Journal of the Oriental Society of Australia (JOSA) 27–28
   (1995–1996); also translated by Mabel Lee as "Without Isms" in
   The Case for Literature (2006).

"Wo shuo ciwei", *Xiandai shi* (Spring 1994); reprinted in *Zhoumo sichongzou* (1996); translated by Gilbert C. F. Fong as "I Say Porcupine" in *Cold Literature: Selected Works by Gao Xingjian* (2005).

"*Meiyou zhuyi* zixu" (1995), in *Meiyou zhuyi* (1996); translated by Mabel Lee as "Author's Preface to *Without Isms*" in *The Case for Literature* (2006).

Gao Xingjian xiju liuzhong (Dijiao, Taipei, 1995).

Mingcheng, in *Gao Xingjian xiju liuzhong* (1995).

Yeyou shen, in *Gao Xingjian xiju liuzhong* (1995); translated by Gilbert C. F. Fong as *Nocturnal Wanderer*, in *The Other Shore: Plays by Gao Xingjian* (1999).

Le Somnambule (Lansman, Carnières-Morlanwelz, 1995).

Ink Paintings by Gao Xingjian, edited by Lee Yulin and translated by D. J. Toman and Tom Smith (Taipei Fine Arts Museum, Taipei, 1995; Homa & Seky, Dumont, New Jersey, 2002).

Zhoumo sichongzou (Xin Shiji, Hong Kong, 1996).

Zhoumo sichongzou, in *Zhoumo sichongzhou* (1996); translated by Gilbert C. F. Fong as *Weekend Quartet* in *The Other Shore: Plays by Gao Xingjian* (1999).

Sheng sheng man bianzou, in *Zhoumo sichongzou* (1996); translated by Gilbert C. F. Fong as "Variation on 'A Slow Slow Tune'" in *Cold Literature: Selected Works by Gao Xingjian* (2005).

Le Goût de l'Encre (Voix Richard Meier, Montigny-les-Metz, 1996).

"Xiandai hanyu yu wenxue xiezuo" (1996), in *Wenxue de liyou* (Ming Pao, Hong Kong, 2001); translated by Mabel Lee as "The Modern Chinese Language and Literary Creation" in *The Case for Literature* (2006).

Meiyou zhuyi (Cosmos, Hong Kong, 1996).

"Wenxue de jianzheng: dui zhenshi de zuiqui" (The Swedish Academy, Stockholm, 2001); translated by Mabel Lee as "Literature as Testimony: The Search for Truth" (The Swedish Academy, Stockholm, 2001); reprinted in *Witness Literature: Proceedings of the Nobel Centennial Symposium*, edited by Horace Engdahl (World Scientific, New Jersey, London, Singapore and Hong Kong, 2002); also reprinted in *The Case for Literature* (2006).

Au Plus Près du Réel: Dialogues sur l'Ecriture (1994–1997), in conversation with Denis Bourgeois (L'Aube, La Tour d'Aigues, 1997).

Quatre Quatuors pour un Week-end (Lansman, Carnières-Morlanwelz, 1998).

L'Encre et la Lumière de Gao Xingjian (Voix Richard Meier, Montigny-les-Metz, 1998).

The Other Shore: Plays by Gao Xingjian, translated by Gilbert C. F. Fong (Chinese University Press, Hong Kong, 1999).

Yige ren de shengjing (Lianjing, Taipei, 1999); translated by Mabel Lee as *One Man's Bible* (2002).

"Wenxue de liyou" (The Swedish Academy, Stockholm, 2000); reprinted in *Wenxue de liyou* (2001); translated by Mabel Lee as "The Case for Literature" (The Swedish Academy, Stockholm, 2000); reprinted in *The Case for Literature* (2006).

Gao Xingjian, edited by Pan Yaoming (Ming Pao, Hong Kong, 2000).

Soul Mountain, translated by Mabel Lee (HarperCollins, Sydney, New York and London, 2000).

Bayue xue (Lianjing, Taipei, 2000); translated by Gilbert C. F. Fong as *Snow in August* (2003).

Mo yu guang: Gao Xingjian jinzuo zhan/Darkness and Light: An Exhibition of Recent Works by Gao Xingjian (bilingual edition), with introduction by Huang Kuang-nan (Lianjing, Taipei, 2001).

Wenxue de liyou, edited by Peng Jieming (Ming Pao, Hong Kong, 2001).

Gao Xingjian juzuo xuan (Ming Pao, Hong Kong, 2001).

Ling yizhong meixue (Lianhe Wenxue, Taipei, 2001); text translated by Nadia Benabid as *Return to Painting* (HarperCollins, New York, 2002).

Muqin (Lianhe Wenxue, Taipei, 2001).

Gao Xingjian xiju ji (Lianhe Wenxue, Taipei, 2001) (ten volumes).

One Man's Bible, translated by Mabel Lee (HarperCollins, New York, Sydney and London, 2002).

"Biyao de gudu", *Lianhebao* Literary Supplement (1 July 2002); translated by Mabel Lee as "The Necessity of Loneliness" in *The Case for Literature* (2006).

Snow in August, translated with introduction by Gilbert C. F. Fong (Chinese University Press, Hong Kong, 2003).

Gao Xingjian: Ink Paintings, 1983–1993, edited by Curtis L. Carter (Haggerty Museum of Art, Milwaukee, 2003).

Ni Mots ni Signes: Encres de Chine sur Papier (Musée des Tapisseries, Ville d'Aix-en-Provence, 2003).

L'Errance de l'Oiseau (Le Seuil, Paris, 2003).

Le Quêteur de la Mort (Le Seuil, Paris, 2003).

Buying a Fishing Rod for My Grandfather, translated by Mabel Lee (HarperCollins, New York, Sydney and London, 2004).

Kouwen siwang (Lianjing, Taipei, 2004).

Pengyou (Lianhe Wenxue, Taipei, 2004).

Gao Xingjian (Galerie Claude Bernard, Paris, 2004).

Cold Literature: Selected Works by Gao Xingjian/ Leng de wenxue: Gao Xingjian zhuzuo xuan (bilingual edition), translated by Gilbert C. F. Fong and Mabel Lee (Chinese University Press, Hong Kong, 2005).

Gao Xingjian Experience, with foreword and introduction by Kwok Kian Chow (Singapore Art Museum, Singapore, 2005).

The Case for Literature, translated by Mabel Lee (HarperCollins, Sydney, 2006).

Chronology of books about Gao Xingjian

Zhao Yiheng, *Jianli yizhong xiandai chanju: Gao Xingjian yu Zhongguo shiyan xiju* (Guojia tushuguan, Taipei, 1999).

Henry Y. H. Zhao, *Towards a Modern Zen Theatre: Gao Xingjian and Chinese Theatre Experimentalism* (SOAS Publications, London, 2000).

Liu Zaifu, *Gao Xingjian zhuangtai* (Ming Pao, Hong Kong, 2000).

Lin Manshu, ed., *Jiedu Gao Xingjian* (Ming Pao, Hong Kong, 2000).

Kwok-Kan Tam, ed., *Soul of Chaos: Critical Perspectives on Gao Xingjian* (Chinese University Press, Hong Kong, 2001).

Zhou Meihui, *Xuedi chan si: Gao Xingjian zhidao* Bayue xue *xianchang biji* (Lianjing, Taipei, 2002).

Michel Draguet, *Gao Xingjian: Le Goût de l'Encre* (Hazan, Paris, 2002).

Sy Ren Quah, *Gao Xingjian and Transnational Theater* (University of Hawaii Press, Honolulu, 2004).

Liu Zaifu, *Gao Xingjian lun* (Lianjing, Taipei, 2004).

Noël Dutrait, ed., *L'Ecriture Romanesque et Théâtrale de Gao Xingjian* (Le Seuil, Paris, 2006).

Articles in English about Gao Xingjian

Barmé, Geremie, "A Touch of the Absurd: Introducing Gao Xingjian, and His Play *The Bus Stop*", *Renditions* 19–20 (1983), pp. 373–378.

Burckhardt, Olivier, "The Voice of One in the Wilderness",
    Quadrant 44.4 (April 2000), pp. 54–57.

Chan, Sin-wai, "Postscript: On Seeing the Play *Bus Stop*: He Wen's Critique
    in the *Literary Gazette*", *Renditions* 19–20 (1983), pp. 387–392.

Chen, Xiaomei, "*Wildman* Between Two Cultures: Some Paradigmatic
    Remarks on 'Influence Studies'", *Comparative Literature Studies* 29.4
    (1992), pp. 397–416; reprinted in Tam, ed., *Soul of Chaos* (2001).

Fong, Gilbert C. F., "Gao Xingjian and the Idea of Theatre", in Tam,
    ed., *Soul of Chaos* (2001).

— "Marginality, Zen, and Omnipotent Theatre", in *Snow in August*
    (2003).

— "Freedom and Marginality: The Life and Art of Gao Xingjian", in
    Cold Literature: Selected Works by Gao Xingjian (2005).

Kinkley, Jeffrey C., "Gao Xingjian in the Chinese Perspective of Qu
    Yuan and Shen Congwen", *Modern Chinese Literature and Culture*
    14.2 (Fall 2002), pp. 130–163.

Lai, Amy T. Y., "Gao Xingjian's *Monologue* as Metadrama", in Tam, ed.,
    Soul of Chaos (2001).

Larson, Wendy, "Realism, Modernism, and the 'Anti-Spiritual
    Pollution' Campaign", *Modern China* 15.1 (1989), pp. 37–71.

Lee, Gregory, and Dutrait, Noël, "Conversation with Gao Xingjian:
    The First 'Chinese' Winner of the Nobel Prize for Literature",
    China Quarterly 167 (2001), pp. 738–748.

Lee, Mabel, "Without Politics: Gao Xingjian on Literary Creation",
    The Stockholm Journal of East Asian Studies 6 (1995), pp. 17–40.

— "Walking Out of Other People's Prisons: Liu Zaifu and Gao Xingjian
    on Chinese Literature in the 1990s", *Asian and African Studies* 5.1
    (1996), pp. 98–112.

— "Personal Freedom in Twentieth Century China: Reclaiming the Self
    in Yang Lian's *Yi* and Gao Xingjian's *Lingshan*", in *History,
    Literature and Society: Essays in Honour of S. N. Mukherjee*, edited
    by Mabel Lee and Michael Wilding (Sydney Association for Studies
    in Culture and Society, Sydney, 1997).

— "Gao Xingjian's *Lingshan/Soul Mountain*: Modernism and the
    Chinese Writer", *Heat* 4 (1997), pp. 128–143.

— "Gao Xingjian's Dialogue with Two Dead Poets from Shaoxing: Xu
    Wei and Lu Xun", in *Autumn Floods: Essays in Honour of Marián
    Gálik*, edited by Raoul D. Findeisen and R. H. Gassman (Peter
    Lang, Bern, 1998); reprinted in Tam, ed., *Soul of Chaos* (2001).

— "Gao Xingjian on the Issue of Literary Creation for the Modern Writer", *Journal of Asian Pacific Communication* 9.1–2 (1999), pp. 83–96; reprinted in Tam, ed., *Soul of Chaos* (2001).

— "Pronouns as Protagonists: Gao Xingjian's *Lingshan* as Autobiography", *China Studies* 5 (1999), pp. 165–183; reprinted in Tam, ed., *Soul of Chaos* (2001).

— "On Nietzsche and Modern Chinese Literature: From Lu Xun (1881–1936) to Gao Xingjian (b. 1940)", *Literature and Aesthetics: The Journal of the Sydney Society of Literature and Aesthetics* (November 2002), pp. 23–43.

— "Nobel in Literature 2000 Gao Xingjian's Aesthetics of Fleeing", *CLCWeb: Comparative Literature and Culture: A WWWeb Journal* 3.1 (March 2003), http://clcwebjournal.lib.purdue.edu/clcweb03-1/lee03.html.

Li, Jianyi, "Gao Xingjian's *The Bus Stop*: Chinese Traditional Theatre and Western Avant-garde" (M.A. thesis, University of Alberta, Edmonton, 1991).

Lim, Wah Guan, "Plays Without Characters: A Historical Study of Characterization in the Plays of Gao Xingjian" (B.A. Honours thesis, University of New South Wales, Sydney, 2005).

Lin, Sylvia Li-chun, "Between the Individual and the Collective: Gao Xingjian's Fiction", *World Literature Today* 75.1 (Winter 2001), pp. 20–30.

Liu Zaifu, "Afterword to *One Man's Bible*", *Modern Chinese Literature and Culture* 14.2 (Fall 2002), pp. 237–242.

Lodén, Torbjörn, "World Literature with Chinese Characteristics: On a Novel by Gao Xingjian", *The Stockholm Journal of East Asian Studies* 4 (1993), pp. 17–40; reprinted in Tam, ed., *Soul of Chaos* (2001).

Lovell, Julia, "Gao Xingjian, the Nobel Prize, and Chinese Intellectuals: Notes on the Aftermath of the Nobel Prize 2000", *Modern Chinese Literature and Culture* 14.2 (Fall 2002), pp. 1–50.

Ma Sen, "The Theatre of the Absurd in Mainland China: Gao Xingjian's *The Bus Stop*", *Issues and Studies: A Journal of China Studies and International Affairs* 25.8 (1989), pp. 138–148; reprinted in Tam, ed., *Soul of Chaos* (2001).

Moran, Thomas, "Lost in the Woods: Nature in *Soul Mountain*", *Modern Chinese Literature and Culture* 14.2 (Fall 2002), pp. 207–236.

Quah, Sy Ren, "Gao Xingjian and China's Alternative Theatre of the 1980s" (M.Phil. thesis, University of Cambridge, Cambridge, 1997).

— "The Theatre of Gao Xingjian: Experimentation Within the Chinese Context and Towards New Modes of Representation" (Ph.D. thesis, University of Cambridge, Cambridge, 1999).

— "Searching for Alternative Aesthetics in the Chinese Theatre: The Odyssey of Huang Zuolin and Gao Xingjian", *Asian Culture* 24 (2000), pp. 44–66.

— "Space and Suppositionality in Gao Xingjian's Theatre", in Tam, ed., *Soul of Chaos* (2001).

— "Exploration in Action: Gao Xingjian's Theatre in the Context of 1980s China", *Asian Culture* 26 (2002), pp. 80–103.

— "Gao Xingjian: The Playwright as an Intellectual", *Nantah Journal of Chinese Language and Culture* 5.1 (2002), pp. 201–242.

— "Performance in Alienated Voices: Mode of Narrative in Gao Xingjian's Theater", *Modern Chinese Literature and Culture* 14.2 (Fall 2002), pp. 51–98.

Riley, Josephine, and Gissenwehrer, Michael, "The Myth of Gao Xingjian", in *Haishi Zou Hao: Chinese Poetry, Drama and Literature of the 1980s*, edited by Josephine Riley and Else Unterrieder (Engelhard-Ng Verlag, Bonn, 1989); reprinted in Tam, ed., *Soul of Chaos* (2001).

Rojas, Carlos, "Without (Femin)ism: Femininity as Axis of Alterity and Desire in Gao Xingjian's *One Man's Bible*", *Modern Chinese Literature and Culture* 14.2 (Fall 2002), pp. 163–206.

Sauviat, Deborah, "The Challenge to the 'Official Discourse' in Gao Xingjian's Early Fiction" (B.A. Honours thesis, University of Sydney, Sydney, 1996).

Schlumpf, Erin, "A New Way of Seeing, A New World to Rule: Elements of Exile in Samuel Beckett's *Fin de Partie* and Gao Xingjian's *Duihua yu fanjie*" (Senior Honours thesis, Dartmouth College, Dartmouth, 2004).

Tam, Kwok-kan, "Drama of Dilemma: Waiting as Form and Motif in *The Bus Stop* and *Waiting for Godot*", in *Studies in Chinese–Western Comparative Drama*, edited by Yun-Tong Luk (Chinese University Press, Hong Kong, 1990).

— "Gao Xingjian, the Nobel Prize and the Politics of Recognition", in Tam, ed., *Soul of Chaos* (2001).

— "Gao Xingjian and the Asian Experimentation in Postmodernist Performance", in Tam, ed., *Soul of Chaos* (2001).

— "Language as Subjectivity in *One Man's Bible*", in Tam, ed., *Soul of Chaos* (2001).

— "Drama of Paradox: Waiting as Form and Motif in *The Bus Stop* and *Waiting for Godot*", in Tam, ed., *Soul of Chaos* (2001).

Tay, William, "Avant-garde Theatre in Post-Mao China: *The Bus Stop* by Gao Xingjian", in *Worlds Apart: Recent Chinese Writing and Its Audiences*, edited by Howard Goldblatt (M. E. Sharpe, New York, 1990); reprinted in Tam, ed., *Soul of Chaos* (2001).

Xu, Gang Gary, "My Writing, Your Pain, and Her Trauma: Pronouns and (Gendered) Subjectivity in Gao Xingjian's *Soul Mountain* and *One Man's Bible*", *Modern Chinese Literature and Culture* 14.2 (Fall 2002), pp. 99–129.

Yan, Haiping, "Theatrical Impulse and Posthumanism: Gao Xingjian's 'Another Drama'", *World Literature Today* 75.1 (Winter 2001), pp. 21–29.

Yip, Terry Siu-han, "A Chronology of Gao Xingjian", in Tam, ed., *Soul of Chaos* (2001).

Yip, Terry Siu-han, and Tam, Kwok-kan, "Gender and Self in Gao Xingjian's Three Post-exile Plays", in Tam, ed., *Soul of Chaos* (2001).

Zou, Jiping, "Gao Xingjian and Chinese Experimental Theatre" (Ph.D. thesis, University of Illinois, Urbana-Champaign, Illinois, 1994).

Céline Yang

Gao Xingjian (b. Ganzhou, Jiangxi Province, China, 4 January 1940) majored in French literature at the Beijing Foreign Languages Institute, graduating in 1962, and was then assigned work as a translator and editor in the Foreign Languages Press, Beijing (1962–79). During the Cultural Revolution (1966–76) he burned the manuscripts of the plays, poems, short fiction and essays that he had written over two decades. In 1980 the first of his many short works of fiction and critical essays began to appear in literary publications, and in the same year he was appointed writer at the People's Arts Theatre in Beijing. In 1982 his book *Preliminary Explorations into the Art of Modern Fiction* was banned and criticised for promoting "decadent" Western modernism, and in 1983 his play *Bus Stop* was banned after a few performances and he was barred from publishing until the following year. In 1985 his play *Wild Man* was staged, but in 1986 his play *The Other Shore* was banned while being rehearsed.

Gao Xingjian played a critical role in introducing modern European writings to China in the early 1980s, as the ban on foreign literature was slowly lifted. He published analytical essays such as "The Agony of Postmodernist French Literature" and "Prévert: French Modernist People's Poet" as well as introductory essays on Beckett, Atonin Artaud, Sartre, Camus, and the Polish playwrights Jerzy Grotowski and Tadeusz Kantor. His translations from the French include Jacques Prévert's *Paroles* (1984) and Eugene Ionesco's *La Cantatrice Chauve* (1985).

While travelling in Europe in late 1987, he made the decision not to return to China, and by the end of the year he had relocated to Paris: he wanted the freedom to fully express his literary and artistic impulses. His creative output successfully expanded in drama, fiction and art, and he became a French citizen in 1997. The French acknowledged his contribution to literature soon after he took residence in France and he was honoured as Chevalier de l'Ordre des Arts et des Lettres in 1992. In 2000 he received three prestigious honours — the Feronia Literature Prize, the Nobel Prize for Literature, and the title of Chevalier of the Order of the Legion of Honour — and in 2002 he received the American Academy of Achievement Golden Plate Award in Dublin.

Gao Xingjian's major writings have been translated into various languages, and his plays have been performed on all continents. Since winning the Nobel Prize, his novel *Soul Mountain* has been published in thirty-four languages. His English-language publications include: *The Other Shore: Plays by Gao Xingjian* (1999); two novels, *Soul Mountain* (2000) and *One Man's Bible* (2002); a book on his aesthetics, *Return to Painting* (2002); a collection of short stories, *Buying a Fishing Rod for My Grandfather* (2004); and this volume of essays, *The Case for Literature* (2006).

Lisa Giles

Mabel Lee (b. Warialda, New South Wales, Australia, 24 December 1939) obtained her Ph.D. in Chinese at the University of Sydney, where she was a member of the academic staff for thirty-four years (1966–2000). Now an honorary associate in the School of Languages and Culture at the University, she continues to work in her field, modern China's intellectual history and literature, and on her literary translations. As well as *The Case for Literature* (2006), she has translated Gao Xingjian's novels *Soul Mountain* (2000) and *One Man's Bible* (2002), and his short-story collection *Buying a Fishing Rod for My Grandfather* (2004). She has also translated three books of poetry by Yang Lian, winner of the 1999 Flaiano International Literature Prize for Poetry: *Masks and Crocodile* (1990), *The Dead in Exile* (1990) and *Yi* (2002). In 2001 she was awarded the New South Wales Premier's Prize for Translation and the PEN Medallion. In 2003 she received the Centenary of Federation Medal "for service to Australian society and literature" and the University of Sydney Alumni Award "for her commitment to the promotion of Asian scholarship and creativity in Australia", and in 2004 she became an Honorary Fellow of the Australian Academy of Humanities.